Winston Churchill

MEMORIES AND TRIBUTES BROADCAST BY THE BBC

Sir Winston Churchill: *study by Karsh of Ottawa*

A SELECTION FROM THE
BROADCASTS GIVEN IN MEMORY OF

Winston Churchill

K.G.,O.M.,C.H.

IN THE SOUND AND TELEVISION

SERVICES OF THE

BRITISH BROADCASTING

CORPORATION

24 to 30 January 1965

British Broadcasting Corporation

Acknowledgement is due to the following for permission to reproduce illustrations:
RADIO TIMES HULTON PICTURE LIBRARY for the illustrations on pages 14 (top right and bottom), 16, 18, 27, 30, 33 (left), 40, 53, 66, 73 and 96;
NATIONAL PORTRAIT GALLERY for the illustration on page 133 (bottom);
IMPERIAL WAR MUSEUM for the illustrations on pages 23, 39, 42, 43, 46, 51, 74, 99, 100, 118 and 127;
A. F. KERSTING for the illustrations on pages 12, 115 and 133 (top)

© British Broadcasting Corporation 1965

First Published 1965

Published by the British Broadcasting Corporation,
35 Marylebone High Street,
London, W.1

Printed in England by
W. S. Cowell Limited, at the Butter Market, Ipswich   No. 6114

Contents

Illustrations

Foreword

by the Rt Hon. LORD NORMANBROOK, G.C.B., Chairman of the
Board of Governors, the British Broadcasting Corporation

IN 1940, soon after he became Prime Minister, Mr Churchill issued the following
order to the War Cabinet Secretariat:

> Let it be very clearly understood that all directions emanating from me
> are made in writing or should be immediately afterwards confirmed in writing.

When I served him as a member of his personal staff, during the war and again
from 1951 to 1955, it was my duty to see that this order was carried out. Today
I feel it is consistent with my old duty to see that the words which were spoken
in memory of him in BBC broadcasts following his death are equally 'confirmed
in writing'. The purpose of this book is to put them permanently on record.

In carrying out this last duty to him, as one of his former secretaries, I believe
that I am also meeting the wishes of many, in this country and overseas, who
would like to have a lasting reminder of what they heard on the air in these
memorial programmes.

With his wife: a photograph taken at Downing Street for his 77th birthday in 1951

Introduction

by MAURICE ASHLEY

THE State funeral of Sir Winston Churchill, as televised from London on 30 January 1965, was watched by many millions of people and broadcast reports of it were heard by millions more. The BBC has since received a vast number of letters from ordinary people at home and abroad who wished in some way to express their gratitude for the services rendered to the free world by this great man and their satisfaction with the way in which he was honoured on their behalf by the Queen and the Government of the nation. Once again television enabled a great many people to share in a noble occasion. When another famous British statesman, William Ewart Gladstone, died and was accorded similar honours, only a limited number – though they came from far and wide – could actually be present at the ceremonies and the funeral. To take an active part is always to pay the highest tribute of all, but there are many who cannot possibly do so. Nevertheless, the third of a million people who queued in the cold and rain to walk past Sir Winston's catafalque as it lay in Westminster Hall in the last week of January showed even more than any words or pictures could do how deeply people felt about his death. Those who have visited his grave at Bladon also testified to their love for him.

Churchill lived a long and remarkable life. He was already twenty-three when Gladstone (who lived to be eighty-nine) received his State funeral and was buried in Westminster Abbey. At the time when Churchill began his career first as a soldier and then as a journalist the only means of disseminating accounts of public events was the newspapers, but the popular press, as it is known today, which began with the halfpenny *Daily Mail*, had not yet even been started. Mass communications and mass entertainment are the invention of the past fifty or sixty years.

9

In an essay, included in his book *Thoughts and Adventures* published at the beginning of the thirties, Winston Churchill reflected upon 'Mass effects in modern life' with that frequent touch of irony he so much enjoyed:

The newspapers (he wrote) do an immense amount of thinking for the average man and woman. In fact they supply him with such a continuous stream of standardized opinion, borne along upon an equally inexhaustible flood of news and sensation, collected from every part of the world every hour of the day, that there is neither the need nor the leisure for personal reflection. All this is but a part of a tremendous educating process. But it is an education which passes in at one ear and out at the other. It is an education at once universal and superficial. It produces enormous numbers of standardized citizens, all equipped with regulation opinions, prejudices and sentiments according to their class or party . . .

But he went on to say, with his usual fairness and sympathy:

It may eventually lead to a reasonable, urbane and highly serviceable society. It may draw in its wake a mass culture enjoyed by countless millions, to whom such pleasures were formerly unknown.

Churchill, who at least up to 1939 was a regular contributor to newspapers and magazines and understood the power and limitations of the Press as well as most men, was inclined to say, as journalists do, that nothing is so dead as yesterday's newspaper. I myself worked for him as a research assistant during the period in the thirties when he was largely engaged in earning a living from writing for such papers as the *Daily Mail* and *Strand Magazine*. He did not always himself take the same trouble over producing articles as he did over preparing a book or a speech: I remember how sometimes he would even dictate them as he was driven from Westerham to Westminster in his motor car. He believed that mass communications and effects were to some extent the characteristic of more backward and primitive communities. He valued the individual above the mass. In that same essay he wrote: 'I have no hesitation in ranging myself with those who view the past history of the world mainly as the tale of exceptional human beings, whose thoughts, actions, qualities, virtues, triumphs, weaknesses and crimes have dominated the fortunes of the race.' Of course since he wrote that, he proved himself beyond question to be one of those 'exceptional human beings'.

In his younger days Churchill led too full and too active a life to spend much of it listening to the radio, though he realized its importance, and when the war of 1939–1945 came he used it as an instrument for his oratory and a means towards victory. We know too that during the war and since he enjoyed seeing films as a form of relaxation (General Eisenhower describes the showing of films at Chequers on page 119) and that he watched television programmes in his retirement. When he was in New York once after the war he remarked (see page 28 below): 'This television has come to take its place in the world; as a rather old-fashioned person I have not been one of its principal champions.' But his mind was too far-ranging and too imaginative not to grasp its use and the pleasures it gives to many.

In this book has been collected together some of the biographical material that was put out by the BBC over the air after Churchill's death on 24 January, a number of the broadcast tributes which were paid to him both from at home and abroad, and a choice of the more vivid impressions by those who really knew him. Inevitably when a man has lived to be ninety, many of his friends themselves are very old or have passed on; but the moment of recollection can in fact be seized and preserved, and under the stress of emotion sometimes the memory will select what is most accurate or endearing. Naturally a great deal of what was broadcast, as of what was written, was ephemeral and even superficial. Print also can turn to platitude what did not seem so when it was spoken at time of stress. This does not aim therefore to be a complete representation of all the tributes from all over the world and from all sorts of people on the air, though the attempt has been made to keep it balanced, sensible, and intelligible. An effort has been made also to avoid too much overlapping. For example, not all the descriptions of Churchill's writing from the numerous people who helped him in his historical work are included; nor are all the tributes by those observers who listened to him speaking in the House of Commons. The book concludes with an article describing some of the many letters that the BBC received from abroad after his death.

The book aims to be a modest contribution to history, the record of a unique occasion. We shall need to await the definitive life by his son before reaching an assessment of Churchill's total career and achievement, unaffected by our own immediate feelings. One might add, however, that Churchill himself bequeathed a great deal of autobiographical material of one kind or another: his history books, as Alan Bullock points out (page 52 below), are highly personal. Churchill once observed to me that he had not left much for his biographers to mop up. But naturally there must be a lot of unpublished material. Yet the memories of his contemporaries that are printed here give the objective touch of really close and informed observers.

One believes in fact that quite an amount of fascinating material is collected in this book: the character and habits, the temper and wit, the tastes and hobbies of Churchill are all set out by those who knew him intimately. Churchill's work in the war is described by leading men like General Eisenhower, Lord Attlee, and Earl Mountbatten; it is delineated too by those on whom he placed the utmost reliance as public servants – such as Lord Ismay, Lord Bridges, and Sir Ian Jacob. His achievements and methods as a historian are put into perspective by Alan Bullock and John Plumb or by men who assisted him such as F. W. Deakin and Alan Hodge. His pleasure in painting is remembered by General Eisenhower, a fellow amateur, and by a professional, Sir Gerald Kelly. But perhaps what stands out most clearly as his largest contribution to history was his work as a statesman and, above all, as a House of Commons man. He loved the House of Commons from his youth upwards; he was in the end to become the Father of the House; he was to receive a unique tribute when he retired from it. All that is recalled in these pages. One of the finest tributes of all comes from the late Lord Morrison of Lambeth, for years one of his political opponents and the participant in many a fierce political debate with him. Lord Morrison said in a 'Panorama' programme: 'Without question he was the one man to be the war-time Prime Minister' (page 61). Few will dissent from that judgment. That is why those of us who lived through that war will honour his memory as long as we live.

The Long Library at Blenheim with its organ

A BIOGRAPHY

A Life of Turbulence and Achievement

by PATRICK O'DONOVAN

This is the edited script of a programme broadcast in BBC Television on 24 January 1965

WINSTON CHURCHILL was born on 30 November 1874. His death sets an end to a life of turbulence and triumph. He wrote and he made history. He got more out of life than any man of his time. It was a rare, a marvellous life.

He was born into the slow-moving world of Queen Victoria. The present seemed excellent, the future assured. He was born into a society dominated by hereditary privilege – ceremonious, exclusive, money conscious – a society that accepted leisure and pleasure as its right. He was born in the Palace of Blenheim at Woodstock, built by the nation for his great ancestor, the first Duke of Marlborough. It was the grandest country house in England. It boasted an organ room that could have served as a cathedral. It celebrated military triumph. But, away from the state apartments and the tapestried saloons, Winston was born in a Victorian room on the ground floor.

His father, Lord Randolph Churchill, was the most brilliant politician of his age. Chancellor of the Exchequer and Leader of the House of Commons, he fought to modernize the Tory Party. He failed at the last to achieve his political ambitions, and he died, still comparatively young, a deeply disappointed man. His mother, Jennie Churchill, was an American by birth. She was both lively and beautiful and men used to say she had the most musical voice they had ever heard.

But although he was born to especial privilege, the story of his childhood reads no differently from that of other little boys of prosperous Victorian families. He went to a private school, where he did not do very well; then he went to Harrow where he in no way distinguished himself – except for a certain impatience of authority. A life-long friend, Sir Shane Leslie, said this about him:

> I believe I must be the only person alive who really remembers Sir Winston as a schoolboy. I have a photograph – a group – taken in Brighton in 1889, of Sir Winston's mother and my mother, and their third sister, showing all the cousins. Later at Banstead manor near Newmarket our great employment was being drilled in Winston's army. There were some eight of us, and the gardeners' boys. It was an army that never changed its commander, and for the ranks there was no promotion. But we dug and built a mud fortification which we called 'The Den'. There was a drawbridge over the moat, and there we sat in perfect happiness and much mud, waiting – as Winston said – for the enemies of England. We really had to wait fifty years, but we were ready.

*The parents of
Winston Churchill:*

*Lord Randolph
Churchill*

*Lady Randolph
Churchill (née
Jennie Jerome)*

*As a subaltern in the
4th Hussars: on his
polo-pony in India,
1896*

Churchill was destined for the army and he went to the Royal Military College at Sandhurst, as a gentleman cadet.

Of course at Sandhurst (continued Sir Shane) he didn't get a literary education. That was the first time he came to himself, he felt a man, he passed in low, he passed out high.

He became a subaltern in the 4th Hussars; and it was then that those strange processes that set some men apart began to stir. He saw his first battle in Cuba, where, simply for the adventure, he served with the Spanish forces in a local civil war.

He managed, by pleading and wangling, to take part in five separate wars before the age of twenty-five. He left his regiment in Bangalore and went campaigning on the North-west frontier. Here he fought wild tribesmen who had no taste for imperial order. He was cut off from the main body by Pathans, who jabbed at him with spears. He used his revolver and escaped unhurt.

In the Sudan a few months later he joined Kitchener's army just before the battle of Omdurman, in which the multitudinous followers of a Moslem holy man were routed. He took part in the famous charge of the 21st Lancers, and it was probably the last cavalry charge in history. These were the high, heady days of Empire.

Still hungry for action, he went off to the South African war as a war correspondent, and he earned money by writing about his campaigns. He joined an armoured train that was wrecked and captured by the Boers. He was made a prisoner of war. He escaped and his captors offered £25 for his return.

He wrote a book about this adventure and it made him famous. It also paid for his election expenses at Oldham where he was elected as a returning hero and a Tory.

But soon the new member fell out with his party over Joseph Chamberlain's policy of Empire Preference and Protection. Unabashed, he wanted no change in old fiscal systems that he thought were good. So he upped and quit his party and the Liberals welcomed their fierce and famous young recruit.

In 1908 he was married to Clementine Hozier – that at least lasted the rest of his life.

Soon he became a member of the Cabinet as Home Secretary. But in the East End of London, in Sidney Street, a handful of anarchists barricaded themselves in a house. Shooting began. The police set siege to them. The Guards were called out. London, and Churchill, had seen nothing like this. He left the decorum of his office to take charge, but a far greater responsibility was now to be given him. He was summoned by war rather than a criminal skirmish. Churchill was appointed First Lord of the Admiralty as war with Germany grew closer. And when war came, the British Fleet, at least, was trained, equipped, mobilized, ready.

As a member of the Cabinet, he tried to play his part in the whole conduct of the war. Against determined opposition from his colleagues and advisers, he decided that the Dardanelles were the back door to victory. The expedition was sent. Success would have destroyed Turkey, perhaps kept Russia fighting in the north. Two years of unnecessary war might have been avoided. But the support he wanted was not given to the men ashore. It ended in heroic and costly disaster. It cast a shadow over Churchill's name. He had still to learn the hard lesson of war that sound plans and high courage are of no use without the resolve and the power to see them through.

Impatient and angry, he resigned from a government that had lost its purpose. He took command of a battalion of the Royal Scots Fusiliers in the trenches and the warrior in him had its fill. But a new, dynamic Prime Minister, Lloyd George, brought him back as Minister of Munitions. Churchill accelerated production. He made his full contribution to the final victory.

With the rest of the world, he joined in the careless rejoicing over the return of peace.

As First Lord of the Admiralty: with Lord Fisher, 1913

But now he had reached that eminence in public life which brings fame and honour and occasional eccentric distinctions in its train. He was elected by the students to the do-nothing post of Lord Rector of Aberdeen University, he was cheered and chaired in the traditional manner. These are the small rewards of public service and they were always very sweet to Churchill.

In Lloyd George's post-war Coalition Government, Churchill became Secretary of State both for War and Air. Now he was responsible for the fledgling Air Force. (It was a decent and leisured introduction to what later would become a fiercely effective partnership in the Battle of Britain.) It was due to his maddening persistence in committee and Cabinet that the tanks had been developed to astonish the enemy in the First World War.

In 1926 came the General Strike. Churchill was by this time a member of Baldwin's Conservative Government. He was an open, unabashed and most active opponent of the strikers. He detested socialism. The Liberals were apparently fading into history. He now believed that the Conservative Party was the only effective political alternative to Labour. So Baldwin brought him in as Chancellor of the Exchequer. During the strike, Churchill cheerfully reverted to journalism. He edited the government newspaper: the *British Gazette*.

He retired to his country house, Chartwell, to paint and to watch the world. He had resigned over a disagreement with Baldwin. Painting was a comfortable pastime during the thirties when he was not only out of office but in fierce opposition to the appeasement and uncertainty in Britain's European policy. These years also allowed him to turn again to the writing of history – this time a massive life of his ancestor, the Duke of Marlborough, who had led an earlier alliance in Europe. One who knew him well as a writer was Sir Harold Nicolson, who said:

> I remember once his saying to me that every politician ought to have a book on hand, and he said that what happened with him was that he would get away from the turmoil and the chatter and the bluster of Westminster, and get down to Chartwell and there he would go into his study and there would be the blotter and there would be the book, and there would be the green lamp, and there would be the manuscript which he'd left off writing a week before – the last Sunday. And he said: 'It's just like having a spaniel to greet one. And I sit down with pleasure and the sound and chatter of Westminster recedes into the background. And in stalk Marlborough and the great figures of the past. And there I am alone in my own room, with my own book.

Churchill as Home Secretary, in the witness box giving evidence on the Sidney Street siege, 1911

Just like a spaniel . . . just like a spaniel,' he said. I can hear him saying it now
– amused – sentimental – regretful for the past.

His real value, I think, to English literature was his historical studies – not
only Marlborough – his books on the second war – six volumes they are, really
magnificent work; of course, I know he was helped and checked and guided
and amused, and befriended by Lord Ismay, when writing those books, but it's
mostly Churchill. And every now and then – even when he's doing the dullest,
grimmest narrative, a question of logistics and all the things that bore the lay-
man like myself, suddenly there comes one of his illuminating spurts which
burst up like an oil well in the desert, throwing smoke and cloud and flashes of
red fire into the air – it really is amazing, when his literary power gets control
of his descriptive power, and bursts into the sky.

In Germany, the antagonist grew like a weed. The evil was prepared. And the
climax for which Churchill's life had been a preparation, moved closer, inevitable
now, more terrible and more squalid than any that faced his ancestor, the peri-
wigged Duke.

Throughout the thirties, it was Churchill who warned the West of evil men.
He spoke. He wrote. He nagged. He lost friends. He gained a reputation for
irresponsible ambition. They spoke as clearly as he. *They* flourished. Churchill
stayed in the wilderness. *He* was right.

It came in 1939: another war, but a war to top all others: a national war that
involved *all* of the nation, a war for survival. A war that changed the nature of
Britain and set Churchill apart in history.

He returned as First Lord of the Admiralty. The choice was inevitable. A
signal was sent to the Fleet – 'Winston is back'. For the first few months the war
was fought for the most part at sea. The land waited. Churchill spoke, with relish,
of his part of the battle:

> But the Royal Navy had immediately attacked the U-boats and is hunting
> them night and day, I will not say without mercy, because God forbid we
> should ever part company with that, but, at any rate, with zeal and not
> altogether without relish.

In April, 1940, the Germans fell upon neutral Norway and Denmark. Our
attempts to intervene ended in utter failure, and the Government's conduct of the
war came under heavy fire in Parliament from all sides of the House. Neville
Chamberlain resigned and Churchill became Prime Minister and Minister of
Defence at a desperate moment in the history of his country.

His Chief of Staff, General (later Lord) Ismay, described the kindling of the
nation:

> To the members of his Government, he said: 'I have nothing to offer you
> but blood, toil, tears, and sweat.' To Britain at large, he proclaimed: 'You ask,
> What is our policy? I will say: It is to wage war by sea, land and air, with all our
> might and with all the strength that God can give us. . . . You ask, What is our
> aim? I can answer in one word: Victory.' . . . But even before he had formed his

Government, the German onslaught fell upon France and the Low Countries. Churchill flew to Paris at once. His uppermost aim was to help France in her agony. But as the front collapsed and the German armour swept onwards like a scythe, Churchill foresaw before anyone else the possibility of an emergency evacuation from the coast. In a few days, escape across the sea was the only hope. Calais was the crux. The garrison there was ordered to fight it out to the end, without support and without relief. The sacrifice of Calais was not in vain. Nearly 340,000 British and French troops were brought back from Dunkirk.

But even as the nation breathed a sigh of relief, Churchill sounded a stern warning. 'Wars are not won by evacuations,' he said. A ceaseless flow of instructions went forth. The island must be put in a state of defence. The army must be reorganized and re-equipped. Counter-offensives across the Channel must be mounted. Leopard brigades must be prepared to harry the enemy. The ardour of his soul set the whole kingdom on fire. Once or twice a week, Churchill visited the threatened sectors himself, to see for himself where everything was, how everything was getting on, and how one thing fitted into another, and to gauge the spirit of the fighting troops and the people, though this he never doubted.

Our own fate and the fate of the world depended on our victory in the air. If we can keep command of the air over our island, he told the French Government at Briare when they were begging us to send them more fighter support, we will win it all back for you. On July 10, the Battle of Britain opened. September 15 was the climax. It was touch-and-go. But as we left the headquarters of No. 11 Fighter Group, late that evening, we felt sure somehow that a great victory had been won. Churchill sat silent in his car for a few minutes, and then, almost to himself, he uttered the words which he later repeated, and which will live for ever:

'Never in the field of human conflict was so much owed by so many to so few.'

As we know, Churchill's voice, broadcast from London in our darkest hour, gave hope and comfort to millions under the Nazi yoke throughout Europe. Bombardment by night followed the attacks by day. As was his wont, Churchill used to go and see for himself. When the news arrived that London docks had been terribly hard hit the previous night, Churchill went straight to the scene. Everywhere the people surged round him shouting 'Good old Winnie!' 'Give it 'em back – we can take it!' 'Poor people,' he said to me, 'poor people. They trust me, and I have given them nothing but disaster.' Nevertheless, his own conviction of ultimate victory was never shaken.

In August 1941, the battleship *Prince of Wales* took Churchill to meet President Roosevelt. They met on the Atlantic. America was not at war, but from this meeting came the Atlantic Charter. It was a declaration of common principles upon which the two countries based their hope for the future. It is still cited as something above the rut of international declarations.

In the years that followed, Churchill travelled the world to meet the allied

Talking to some of the troops who led the assault on D-Day when he visited Caen, 1944. On the right is General Sir Bernard Montgomery

leaders – Washington, Cairo, Moscow, Casablanca, Teheran, Quebec, Yalta. Meetings like the one with Stalin were remembered by Churchill's Chief of the Imperial General Staff, Lord Alanbrooke:

As C.I.G.S., I think probably one of the things I remember most was Churchill's determination whenever he possibly could to establish contact with all those connected with the war, and I think probably his visit to Moscow at a very early stage, to see Stalin, was one of the bravest things he did. Because it was at a moment when it was quite impossible for us to establish a Western front here in Europe, and yet he went there to see them. I remember well the first interview that we had, or rather the second interview because I wasn't there myself at the first one – I arrived in time for the second one which was the one when things got heated: Stalin got up smoking this bent pipe of his and started saying to Winston 'When are you going to start fighting? If you start fighting you'll find it's not too bad, we've been fighting now for some time while you've been looking on. Aren't you going to start soon?' And this came through the interpreter, who was rather raw at his job probably and he sneered at Winston, and said to him 'Are you never going to start fighting?' Of course it was like a red rag to a bull, Winston came down with a crash on the table, and then flowed from him the most wonderful oration, which started off with the lines which I always remember to this day: 'If it wasn't for the fighting quality shown by the Red Armies at Stalingrad –' and then it went on:

*The Potsdam
Conference, July
1945: linking hands
with President
Truman and
Marshal Stalin*

'Sir, I tell you what I think of you, the whole lot of you –' in the same high standard. Stalin stopped smoking and a broad grin came over his face, and before this could be interpreted, he held out his hand like that and then he spoke back again: he said: 'I don't understand what you're saying, but by God, I like your sentiment.'*

Churchill believed passionately in the idea that the United States was the proper and decent and inevitable ally for Britain. But beyond the journeys and that deathly responsibility for war, he relished most a visit to the men and the leaders in the field. In North Africa and later in Italy, he went to see for himself and to use his influence. To the men whose bodies had to endure and express his plans in action, Churchill was the only tolerable leader. This pleasure-loving, aging and splendid man was trusted as no other man was trusted by these men at war. He brought inspiration and confidence to the fighting men in whose hands lay the success or failure of the grand designs for victory.

Men took a peace-time delight in his arrogance in the face of odds, in the uncomplicated but understood symbolism of the 'V' sign. Men in fear, men in danger, men at war recognized a colleague and an experienced practitioner – not another politician or general.

Back in London, either in Downing Street or in the secret underground head-quarters in Storey's Gate, Churchill and his Cabinet colleagues controlled the life of a people at war. The Prime Minister had his private room underground, where he could sleep after working, and, abhorring the unfriendly morning, he chose

*Cf. the story related by Mr Averell Harriman on page 91.

22

The Mulberry harbour: inshore end of one of the piers being placed in position at Arromanches

often to work late into the night. Not far from his bedside, he could be in immediate touch with President Roosevelt. This drab and closely-guarded fortress saw much of the planning for the biggest operation of all: the invasion of Europe in June 1944.

Churchill had intended to watch the bombardment of the Normandy coast on D-day from one of the cruiser squadrons; and it was only the personal intervention of the King that at last dissuaded him. Four days later, however, when the bridgehead was firmly established, he went across and for the first time in four years set foot on French soil. Two years before, Churchill had demanded 'Piers for use on beaches'. 'They must float up and down with the tide,' he said. 'Let me have the best solution worked out. Don't argue the matter. The difficulties will argue for themselves.' The result was the Mulberry harbour at Arromanches, later to be called Port Winston. Once more Churchill followed the long hard road that took his troops through France and across the Rhine to Berlin.

The end of the war in Europe brought scenes of tumultuous rejoicing in Britain. 'Weary and worn, impoverished but undaunted, and now triumphant,' wrote Churchill, 'we had a moment that was sublime.' To the exultant people, Churchill stood for all that had brought them through the dark years to victory. It was his moment of utter and temporary triumph.

Europe was free and it paused in its rejoicing to acclaim Churchill. His voice, his confident eccentricity, his arrogant and civilized contempt for the enemy had given them hope when hope seemed irrational. In Paris he was given the highest honour of France. One after another the cities of liberated Europe paid their willing tribute to the man. No shadow from the future marred that deserved triumph. In a Berlin without Hitler, he took the salute of the troops he had visited so often on the long and bloody road to this place. With him were some of the commanders who had survived his impatience and some of his colleagues in the coalition government that had shared the burden. But the coalition government had ended; a general election had been promised to the country as one of the immediate fruits of peace. Three weeks of uncertainty while the overseas military votes were counted. Not knowing the basis of his authority, Churchill went to Potsdam. Here for the first time he met President Truman. His old friend, Roosevelt, had died a month before victory.

This was Stalin's last meeting with the men he used as allies. Churchill was already worried by the Soviet drift back towards hostility to the West. He wanted the West to keep the strength, to negotiate from strength with a man who only understood power. He was to leave deeply dissatisfied.

Of the three who sat together at Potsdam, two would remain in power for the next crucial years, drawing apart in their leadership of East and West. But Churchill, at seventy-one, was to be thrown from office by one more of the violent acts of fate that dominated his career.

The day before the result was announced, Churchill returned to London. He had been deposed. His personal prestige was not enough to save the Tory Party from one of its major defeats. When the cruel war with Japan was over (and he took his place on the King's dais for the Victory Parade in London) he was a shocked man – angry and more than a little bitter. 'All our enemies having surrendered unconditionally, or being about to do so,' he wrote, 'I was immediately dismissed by the British electorate from all further conduct of their affairs.'

It was not Number 10 Downing Street and the role was unfamiliar and uncomfortable. For the first time in his long Parliamentary career, he was the Leader of the Opposition.

When the time came to restore the House of Commons, ruined by German bombs, Mr Attlee was Prime Minister. Churchill, standing beside him to see the stone laid, must have remembered his proud vow – seven years earlier – given among the smoking ruins. 'It must be rebuilt, just as it was.'

Out of office he dreamt again of a united Europe. He was one of the progenitors of the idea of a Europe restored, willing and able to act, supplying to the world its own brand of wisdom. . . .

It is not a movement of parties but a movement of people. And we must endeavour by passionate and faithful service to prepare for the day when there will be an effective world government resting upon the main groupings of mankind. I hope to see a Europe where men of every country will think as much of being a European as of belonging to their native land. *Mesdames et Messieurs prenez garde, je vais parler français.* . . .

The people, the ordinary people of Europe welcomed him as among their supreme liberators and few understood his parliamentary rejection by the British

As a racehorse owner: patting Colonist II after it had won the Florizel Handicap Stakes at Kempton Park, 15 September 1950

electorate. Somehow, he added an extra flesh and dignity and splendour to the brave and sad years they had known. No one doubted, then, that the United Kingdom was part of Europe and foreigners persisted in hoping great things of this man. He was an aristocrat and yet he spoke intimately to the longings of the crowd. In those same years, in the United States, as early as 1946, he advocated a policy of unity backed by strength and he sounded a warning on Eastern Europe.

A shadow (he said) has fallen upon the scenes so lately lighted by the Allied victory. Nobody knows what Soviet Russia and its Communist international organization intends to do in the immediate future . . . From Stettin in the Baltic to Trieste in the Adriatic, an iron curtain has descended across the Continent . . . I do not believe that Soviet Russia desires war . . . From what I have seen of our Russian friends and allies during the war, I am convinced that there is nothing they admire so much as strength and there is nothing for which they have less respect than weakness, especially military weakness.

On a later visit he said:

I must not conceal from you tonight the truth as I see it. It is certain that Europe would have been communized like Czechoslovakia, and London under bombardment some time ago but for the deterrent of the atomic bomb in the hands of the United States.

Back in his home in Kent, Churchill had the time to turn again to the pleasures of literature. He produced the six massive volumes of his war history. They are among the most eloquent works of English literature: a unique and personal memoir by the man who had dominated those times. In 1947, for the first time

25

he sent some paintings to the Royal Academy – anonymously. He was elected Honorary Academician Extraordinary. Even the critics found things to praise in the vivid, attacking quality of his work. Suddenly and typically he emerged in what was a new role for him. It accorded with his past and it was somehow expected of him: a racehorse owner. His most famous horse, Colonist II, was a popular winner.

Churchill plunged into party politics. Though he spoke most often on foreign affairs, again and again he attacked Labour's nationalization programme. This to him seemed mischievous and mad. The life of the first post-war Parliament drew to an end and in February 1950 came the General Election. For some two years, the flood that had swept the Labour Party to victory had been receding. The Tories dared to hope again. The result was very close.

Mr Attlee was returned to office though not to power, with his party's majority cut from 168 to 8; the national verdict was uncertain. So Churchill remained in Opposition, and in readiness, for he was not to be out of office much longer. The difficulties of government with such a meagre majority were insuperable. Another general election alone could solve the problem. And in October 1951, just over eighteen months later, it came.

Churchill had never lost his *personal* popularity. The crowds that watched him move through the election ritual cheered him as they did in the days of assured power. But this bitter lesson was now six years old; party triumph did not, for sure, follow his personal success. He had never yet achieved election as a peace-time Prime Minister. At seventy-seven he still awaited the people's full vote of confidence. Once again the result was very close. Only a few seats were won over by the Conservatives, but they were enough to change the verdict. Churchill was back in Downing Street. Soon afterwards he spoke at the Lord Mayor's banquet in Guildhall:

> This is the first occasion when I have addressed this Assembly here as Prime Minister. The explanation, my Lord Mayor, is convincing. When I should have come as Prime Minister the Guildhall was blown up, and before it was repaired I was blown out.

An opponent was Emanuel Shinwell who remembers him thus:

> When Churchill was Prime Minister in 1952, I asked him a question – I was then sitting on the Front Opposition bench – and he didn't like either the question or the tone. He was a bit furious so we had a row. When it was over I left the Chamber and went into the Library and after a minute or two I came out into the corridor, and saw him coming along, smoking, as usual, a big fat cigar. I tried to dodge him, because I felt a bit embarrassed about this quarrel. But he stopped me and said: 'Hello, have you read the latest news?' So I thought he was going to impart some secret military information. I said: 'No.' He said: 'My horse won today.' 'Oh,' I said, 'you're a nice friend, why didn't you tell me. What price was it?' He said: 'Four to one.' And he turned away laughing. That was the type of man he was.

26

Walking in procession to St George's Chapel, Windsor, to be installed as a Knight of the Garter, June 1954

He was in many ways unpredictable. You'd never be quite sure what was going to happen. . . . I've seen him in the House of Commons, when the Labour members were jeering at him, for some reason or another, often for no reason at all, and he would poke out his tongue at them . . . and, of course, everybody would laugh at this. On other occasions he could be malicious and even rude and offensive. But he was always tolerant and gracious to an opponent if he regarded that opponent as sincere, if he had personal integrity, if he was a man with convictions and principles.

So he resumed the duties of Prime Minister, and, for a time, those of Minister of Defence. He again enjoyed it vastly.

Early in her reign, the Queen gave a personal reward for his long and magnificent service. He became Sir Winston Churchill, Knight Commander of the Most Noble Order of the Garter. And, at Windsor Castle, as the newest of the knights, he walked alone at the head of the procession that made its way to St George's Chapel for the installation ceremony.

His knighthood had been announced in time for the Coronation. On that day, he rode to Westminster Abbey with an escort from his old regiment, the 4th

Hussars. He was, as a historian and a conservative, a man who felt from the heart the reality of the union of past and present. The robes and the ceremonial, though fun in themselves, expressed for him a deeper truth that he had spent his life to serve. He continued his visits to Washington, again as Prime Minister. He had set his heart on a renewal of the war-time idea of informal meetings among the men of power. And later visits brought him again into partnership with President Eisenhower. He believed that the first, best hope for peace lay in the unity of the English-speaking world.

As he said in a speech in Washington:

What is the good of speaking one language if you can't put your differences to each other plainly? That is the great advantage of one language. One language is the biggest thing, as Bismarck said. The greatest development of the nine-teenth century was that the United States was found definitely to speak only the, may I say it, the English language.

That flash of wit often threw out a memorable phrase. He as well as his audience enjoyed it. He once said, at a dinner in London, 'It is my belief that you cannot deal with the most serious things in the world unless you also understand the most amusing'.

This good humour was often spontaneous, as on a New York quayside.

This television (he then said) has come to take its place in the world; as a rather old-fashioned person I have not been one of its principal champions, but I don't think it needs any champions, I think it can make its own way and I think it is a wonderful thing indeed to think that every expression on my face at this moment may be viewed by millions of people throughout the United States. I hope that the raw material is as good as the methods of distribution.

He was not in love with television. But in November 1954, on his eightieth birthday, BBC Television brought him greetings from many friends. Churchill made an unexpected appearance before the cameras to reply.

I am fortunate indeed to have met these men and women and to have worked with them in the years of struggle through which we have passed and I am grateful that modern science has enabled me upon my birthday to receive in this amusing manner their friendly greetings and good wishes.

Earlier that day, members of both Houses of Parliament had gathered in Westminister Hall to pay their birthday tributes. Mr Attlee, his Deputy in the war and then his opponent and successor, presented the gift of the two Houses, saying: 'On behalf of both Houses of Parliament, Mr Prime Minister, I ask you to accept this portrait.' He was not, it is true, much pleased with the modernity of the portrait. Churchill was also given a richly bound book. The Father of the House, Mr Grenfell, made the presentation. His friends of all parties – almost every member of the House of Commons – had signed it. Churchill, much moved, expressed his gratitude:

This is to me the most memorable public occasion of my life. No one has ever received a similar mark of honour before. There has not been anything like it in British history . . . I was very glad that Mr Attlee described my speeches in the war as expressing the will not only of Parliament but of the whole nation. I have never accepted what many people have occasionally said – namely that I inspired the nation. Their will was resolute and, as it proved, unconquerable. It fell to me to express it and if I found the right words, you must remember that I have always earned my living by my pen and by my tongue. It was the nation and the race dwelling all round the globe, that had the lion heart. I had the luck to be called upon to give the roar.

And here, in effect, his public life ended.

Four months later, on 4 April, 1955 the Queen and the Duke of Edinburgh dined as his and Lady Churchill's guests at 10 Downing Street. It was a farewell party. The next afternoon at an audience with the Queen at Buckingham Palace, Churchill tendered the last of his many resignations.

Replying to Mr Attlee's presentation address after he had received, at a ceremony in Westminster Hall, an 80th birthday gift from both Houses of Parliament of a portrait of himself by Graham Sutherland (in background), 30 November 1954. Attlee is seated on the right

M.P. for Oldham
(*photo c.1900*)

Now came the years of real retirement. He travelled. He painted. He rested. He wrote a little. He did not repine or intrigue in the manner of many who have given up power. Even these were to be good years.

Many great men have lived in the old house in Downing Street and, please God, many more will follow them. Only history can say if any of them be greater than Winston Leonard Spencer Churchill.

A PORTRAIT

Soldier, Statesman, Historian

by Christopher Sykes and Maurice Brown

Broadcast in the BBC Home Service 29 January 1965

When a friend once asked Winston Churchill if he ever wished he had taken up some career other than politics he seemed surprised at the question. He exclaimed, 'Certainly not!' but a moment after he added: 'Except, of course, the army.' He began his career in the army, where Sergeant Hallaway knew him as a young subaltern:

The 4th Hussars were stationed in Aldershot in '95 when Mr Churchill joined, and the first I see of him he was walking across the parade ground with Captain Smith, and they made straight for my stables, and he introduced Mr Churchill to me and Mr Churchill walked round the stables with me and the first thing he saw was a man brushing his horse and he says, 'What is that silly man doing?' – 'He is cleaning his horse's tail, the proper thing.' He says, 'Oh, I suppose you are right.' A little farther on there was a man cleaning his horse's hooves out. He said, 'I will do that.' I said, 'No, sir, you don't have to do that; I don't have to do it now I am in charge of the troop.'

Shortly afterwards Churchill was with his regiment on the North-west frontier. General Sir Hubert Gough remembered him in the mess:

We were fairly close to Peshawar, we used to come in sometimes on Saturday evenings and perhaps have a hunt in the morning, and that was the first time that I ever had the opportunity of seeing Winston Churchill. He struck me then as being both ambitious and capable, because he was only a young subaltern in the 4th Hussars. He would come into the big mess which was full of senior officers and standing before the fire would give them quite a dissertation on how the war should be conducted. I thought to myself: 'Well anyhow he is learning to be a great orator and practice certainly ought to make perfect'.

Sergeant Hallaway remembered a conversation:

The Egyptian affair came along you know and he says, 'I am trying to get out to Egypt' and he says, 'and I think there is going to be trouble there'. So eventually he come one morning and he says, 'I am off'.

He was off to the cavalry charge of Omdurman which he was to immortalize in his writings. He returned to his regiment in India and to his last spell of duty as a soldier. Sergeant Hallaway obtained an official reference from him before he left.

I had to go to his bungalow for this reference. He had paper in the typewriter on the table but it was only a bit of tracing paper. When he typed this reference out

– he signed his name; he said 'Of course, my name is nothing now, but it might be some day'.

He left the army; became a newspaper correspondent in the South African War, and in 1900 was elected M.P. for Oldham. In May 1904 he crossed the floor of the House and joined the Liberal Party. From 1906 to 1908 he was Under-Secretary of State for the Colonies. In 1908 he was appointed President of the Board of Trade. In those days such an appointment necessitated an election and Winston Churchill was defeated in North-west Manchester. Sir Garnet Wilson recalls how the young states-man put this setback to rights:

Defeated in Manchester in 1908, Winston Churchill found a ready sanctuary in Dundee, at a by-election then pending. Sanctuary or no, he faced the new contest with an air of self-confident challenge. Trite as may be the saying – he came, he saw, he conquered. He won the hearts of his new constituents at his very first meeting. It was the earliest of many triumphs.

A brilliant career opened: President of the Board of Trade, 1908 to 1910; Home Secretary, 1910 to 1911 in which year he became First Lord of the Admiralty. His personal assistant in that post was Mr Gerald A. Steel who says:

He was exactly what you would expect from his characteristics. He was full of enthusiasm, working up till two or three in the morning, starting at seven o'clock dictating in bed for a couple of hours, then a hot bath and breakfast and then straight into the Admiralty at ten; and from ten he worked all through the day up till two o'clock or three o'clock in the morning, and when he did turn in, strict instructions were given that he was not to be woken up. On one occasion I did wake him up and tell him that there was a rebellion in South Africa, and he was very annoyed and rightly said, 'What can I do about it?' He was like an encaged lion and he kept that all the way through his life. Enormous enthusiasm and every-thing new. The war game was a great invention of his. When he first arrived at the Admiralty I went over the Admiralty Arch with him and he said 'What is there here?' And I said 'This is the Admiralty library,' so he turned to the librarian and said, 'Do the officers use this library much?' And he said 'No, sir, an officer comes in occasionally.' 'Scrap the lot, move them all down to Greenwich, turn the whole of the floor into a map of the North Sea so that we can play the war game.' All to be done in a week. Well, I took the opportunity of telling him that was a rather rapid move and so it wasn't done, and he fortunately realized that this was a bit sweeping.

Prince Louis of Battenberg was the First Sea Lord. His son, Earl Mountbatten, looks back to the days before the First World War:

It was about the time when I joined the navy, as a cadet in 1913, that I first knew Sir Winston Churchill. He was at that time First Lord of the Admiralty and my father was First Sea Lord; so it happened that I would meet him from time to time when I was at home on leave. He was extraordinarily kind to youngsters and I still have clear memories of the flattering way he spoke to me as though I were a fully-fledged naval officer: and I also remember my father talking about him with tremendous admiration and indeed affection, for although he was a great

As First Lord of the Admiralty, with Prince Louis of Battenberg at Dover before the 1914 war

(right)
First World War: wearing a French steel helmet, with officers of the French XXXIII Corps at their H.Q. at Camblain L'Abbé, 1915

deal younger than my father they worked together as a wonderful team and my father was always thrilled to have his stimulating ideas which the naval staff then endeavoured to translate into action. When he came back to the Admiralty at the outbreak of the Second World War I was at sea; I remember with what excitement the Fleet received the signal 'Winston is back'. 'Now we shall get a move on,' everybody said. But it wasn't until Winston Churchill became Prime Minister that we really got going.

The First World War broke out in August 1914 and the time was marked by one of Winston Churchill's most famous deeds. At the end of the summer exercises he did not disperse the Fleet according to the usual routine procedure. To recall Kitchener's words to him: 'There is one thing no one can take from you. The Fleet was ready.' The same could not be said of the Army. One of the unsolved problems of 1914 was how to give military help to the Belgians in their country. General Lord Freyberg recorded his memories of the First Lord's contribution:

Winston started the First World War as First Lord of the Admiralty. When he found that there were several thousand Naval Reservists with no immediate war job, he formed them into the Royal Naval Division and shipped them off posthaste to Antwerp in a desperate last moment attempt to stem the German onrush in Flanders. I joined the Naval Division and found myself in the course of a few hours in a naval hospital in Antwerp with a broken right arm. Winston was there in the uniform of a younger brother of Trinity House.

When we evacuated Antwerp and came back to England, Winston was beset by his friends eager to serve in the Naval Division, and in the Hood battalion we had a corps d'élite of outstanding personalities. My officers in the Hood battalion, most of them Winston's friends, were an entirely exceptional group, each one of whom, had he lived, seemed destined to make his mark. For the most part they were scholars – the 'Latin Club' as the less scholarly called them, while the alternative section became known as 'The Hounds'. The Latin Club included Arthur Asquith, the Prime Minister's second son, Charles Lister, Johnny Dodge, Patrick Shaw Stewart, Cleg Kelly, the musician and composer, and Rupert Brooke, the poet.

In May of 1915 the failure of the Dardanelles expedition forced Winston Churchill's resignation from the Admiralty, and at the end of the year he went out to France as an officer in the army. He served first with the 2nd Grenadier Guards and then as battalion commander of the 6th Royal Scots Fusiliers. A classic description of him as he was then has been recorded by Professor Dewar Gibb:

His coming was not exactly popular with the officers. He was then a prominent Liberal statesman and any politics we had were anything rather than Liberal politics. Nor as an old cavalry officer could he be said to show great knowledge of the details of infantry combat. But all criticism ceased in a matter of days. Our new Colonel meant business and he electrified the battalion. Of course he was unconventional, of course he didn't know how you formed platoon on the left, but what did that matter? He won our hearts by qualities not usually found in officers commanding Kitchener's army battalions in France. He was utterly regardless of danger. He planned odd and interesting exploits. He seemed to revel in war. Not many colonels in a quiet hour could set up their easel and paint – to such good purpose as he did.

But what endeared Churchill to us most of all was his behaviour when it became known that our battalion was to be joined up with a fusilier battalion in another division. Many officers would be 'redundant' as they say today, and their fate uncertain. The Colonel then had a list compiled of what each officer wanted and procuring a car he scoured Northern France for days doing his best for us all. Nothing so well illustrated his sympathy, loyalty and generosity. Only Churchill, we felt, could or would have done it.

He returned to politics and ministerial responsibilities towards the end of the war. In the immediate post-war years, from 1921 to 1922, Winston Churchill achieved statesmanlike success as Colonial Secretary. Sir Gerard Clauson was a member of his staff.

He was no stranger to the Office; he had been Parliamentary Under-Secretary of State from 1905 to 1908, and I suspect that some of my senior colleagues, who had experienced his unconventional methods during that period, viewed his arrival with some measure of apprehension. In fact, however, the ten months that he spent with us were happy and constructive ones. He made it clear from the beginning that while he had a close interest in the affairs of all the Colonies, including the self-governing Colonies – the term Dominions was not invented until two or three years later – his principal object was to set up a Middle East Department.

34

Mr Churchill had a wide circle of friends with interests in that area and almost immediately I found myself removed from the Nigerian Department and put in a room with the man who was probably the most distinguished and certainly the most colourful of them all, T. E. Lawrence.

Mr Churchill always had a warm regard for old friends. Mr, later Sir Edward, Marsh had become his Private Secretary when he was Under-Secretary of State for the Colonies, and had rejoined him in that capacity during the war. He now came back to the Colonial Office as Principal Private Secretary, an arrangement which had one unusual advantage. Mr Churchill was a terrific worker but worked unusual hours; I suspect that a good deal of his work was done in bed. There was an ancient tradition in the Colonial Office, inherited, I believe, from the Byzantine Empire, that only the Secretary of State could write his minutes in red ink and that he could write them in nothing else. Obviously red ink and a steel pen were awkward things to handle in bed; that was where Eddie Marsh came in. It was not long before the officers of the Department came to realize with feelings of delight, amusement, or horror, as their temperaments dictated, that when a paper came back to them, the operative entry on it was not the neat W.S.C. in red ink – that was Eddie Marsh's contribution – but the little tick in red chalk which indicated that the great man had seen and approved the recommendation.

In the General Election of November 1922 Winston Churchill met defeat. He did not return to the House of Commons till 1924. It was a moment of frustration, but, being the man he was, a moment also of abundant private interests. Paul Maze, the French painter, saw much of him.

I remember we met in a mutual friend's house in the South of France and he came up to me and asked what I was doing. 'Well, Winston, I'm painting hard, trying to forget all about the war. And what are you doing?' 'Oh,' he said, 'I'm writing a book on the war.' 'Well, my dear Winston, it's like digging up a cemetery.' 'Yes, but with a resurrection!' he replied. . . .

How he managed to organize his relaxation in painting was a masterpiece in itself. I've seen Winston arrive in France looking worn out after writing hard. I remember that moment when he was writing on Marlborough, and was trying to push one volume through – hard work. He arrived worn out; next day he was in the garden without a hat with the sun shining on his head – he was painting away and, like a flower, blooming again in the atmosphere: absolutely marvellous.

A painting memory comes from Sir Walter Lamb, former Secretary of the Royal Academy ; he was a guest with Winston Churchill at Blenheim Palace:

On 1 June the sun shone benignly and the Duchess, knowing that Churchill would be resolving to do some painting out of doors, suggested that I should go with him and help to find a suitable subject for his brush. He at once asked me to go and when he had donned an overall and a good-sized hat we set forth together. From the cavernous recesses of one of the great vaults in the basement floor of the Palace emerged a great number of liveried footmen, one bearing an easel, another a canvas, another a palette, paints and brushes, another a large umbrella and two others bringing a table furnished with bottles, glasses and cigars. Churchill and I at the head of the procession strolled observantly by the lake and carefully considered the interests of successive points of view.

We finally settled on a spot by a shady tree near the bank where could be studied, beyond pleasant reflections in gleaming and slightly stirred water beneath a willow, a background formed by the park on the far side of the lake. After tasting some of the refreshment on the table and seeing the eager painter with everything ready for an attack on this subject, I left him to his own devices. Having walked some distance away I turned once or twice, and having received a memorable vision of him, cigar in mouth, absorbed in the problems of composition, form, colour, and the rest, and clearly tackling them with great zest and vigour, I returned from my walk in an hour or so and found that he had nearly completed an attractive picture. He seemed glad to have my opinion of what he had done and to know that I liked it and why.

From 1924 to 1929 Winston Churchill was Chancellor of the Exchequer. His policy was criticized and when he fell from office in 1929 he was for ten years in the political wilderness.

A political opponent, Mr Granville Sharp, Q.C., *experienced collisions with Churchill at the hustings:*

He always hit hard and shrewdly in his speeches and written messages to the electors, and he did not take offence if the return blows were hard. He set a pattern for all time on how an election should be fought; and one felt always at such times the importance of trying to follow and live up to his example. Triviality was barred, and if at times one offended, it was followed by a sense of shame.

On one such occasion I had misguidedly said of him in a leaflet that he had sullied the record of West Essex Conservatism by quarrelling with his leaders. When later we met, he refused to shake hands, saying: 'A word stands between us'. I said I would understand better if I knew the word, and when having himself been reminded of it by his wife, he repeated it. He added 'Nasty word.' I said I had not meant more than 'spoilt' and was sorry; and his instant reaction was: 'You have said you are sorry?' I said, 'Yes.' Thanking me, he held out his hand.

That election was in 1935. He was still in the political wilderness, still relying on private life. He forgot his embitterment as far as he could in hard work. He wrote his Life of Marlborough, *and Paul Maze remembers something of that process.*

He was anxious to find the right sentence which would once and for all knock out Macaulay's conception of Marlborough. I can see him now repeating aloud a sentence, bringing in here a word, taking another one out and saying 'Ah, I think now . . . what about this?' Like a sculptor he would smooth the form of his sentence and then in the end feel that he had got hold of something; that was it. No, things were not as easy as people think with his writing; he used to polish every sentence and he would apply to his speeches the same care as he did to every book; everything was really thought out and polished.

He found escape in sport too: Mr Roland Smith remembers a shooting party on the estate of the Duke of Westminster.

The Duke lined up about eight different men who were going to load for the

Churchill the artist: at work on a canvas in Switzerland, 1946

different people who came to shoot. Well, he came along and his first words were, 'Now, Winnie, take your choice'. And they all stood there so old Winnie went along with his frowning eyebrows, you know, and wandered up and down, and he looked at one and grabbed him by the front. He says, 'You'll do', and he pulled him out: this was my friend who was a farmer and great sportsman and ever after he led off Mr Churchill when he came to these shoots at Eaton. Mr Churchill was not a good shot, but the Duke was clever; he always put two good ones to the sides of him and one behind him, and Churchill would bang off, two barrels, and down would come the birds, and he would say 'Got him'. He had not got him – the man behind him had got him. And he used to say 'Got him, got him, that was a good one'. 'You never touched him, sir, it's Lord So-and-So behind you who shot him.' He was just like a big boy on these occasions.

There was some escape in such parties. But there was no escapism in Winston Churchill. Mr Smith gives us compelling evidence.

It would be the winter of 1938 and I remember it was a lovely wintry morning with real sunshine, and when he came out you could see there was something on his mind and he did not alter all the morning; and then after the first drive, after lunch, he sort of exploded to his friends, and we were walking just by the side of him. We heard all the conversation and he was warning everybody that the

37

Germans were preparing for another war and that planes would bomb us and our families and their children – yours and mine. He roared, as if he was in a foul temper, and then he sighed and said 'No one will listen to me, no one will listen to me', which shook me to the core. He seemed so certain about it all, and then the sadness in his voice when he said 'No one will listen to me'.

Less than two years later Winston Churchill was Prime Minister, at one of the most sombre moments of modern history. Lord Ismay, the Chief of Staff to the Minister of Defence, tells of two episodes still vivid in his memory:

June 1940; the scene a bare room in a disused château at Briare on the Loire; the actors, the French and British High Commands, seated round a long table; General Weygand describing the desperate plight of the French army: pleading that all the fighter aircraft in England should be sent to their aid. 'Here,' said the General, 'is the decisive point. Now is the decisive moment. Nothing must be held back, everything must be hurled into the battle.' A terrible moment for Winston Churchill, lover of France, and the most loyal and generous of friends. A long pause and then the measured reply, 'No, this is not the decisive point, nor the decisive moment. That will come when Hitler hurls his bombers against Great Britain. If we can keep command of the air over our islands and if we can keep the seas open, as we certainly shall do, we will win it all back for you.'

Then came a characteristic gesture of chivalry and defiance. 'But if you think it best for France in her agony that her army should capitulate let there be no hesitation on our account. For whatever happens here we shall fight on for ever and ever and ever. I pledge you my word that Britain will never surrender.' M. Reynaud, obviously touched, said: 'But if our army surrenders the whole might of Germany will be turned upon you, and they will invade you, and then what'll you do?' Back whipped the reply: 'I haven't thought that out carefully, but broadly speaking I should propose to drown as many as possible of them on the way over, and then to knock on the head anything that managed to crawl ashore.'

When things were at their blackest in 1940 a crowd of men and women greeted him with cries of 'Good old Winnie, we can take it. Give it 'em back.' His eyes filled with tears. 'Poor people, poor people,' he said. 'They trust me, and I can give them nothing but disaster for a long, long time.'

After the fall of France, there came those unforgettable days when Winston Churchill rallied the people by means of radio. The famous theatrical producer, Michel St Denis, was at that time working in the French Service of the BBC. He remembers collaborating in one of the broadcasts:

'We are waiting for the long-promised invasion; so are the fishes,' said Churchill, in his memorable speech to the French of 21 October 1940. That day, I had the privilege to lunch, dine, and work during most of the afternoon with the Prime Minister, most of the time alone with such a man at such a moment! To begin with, I had to ask him if he would approve a short text of introduction which I had written on instruction from the BBC. He looked at it, and complained that it was too long, that I was saying much too much good about him. 'You know how the French are,' he said, 'they won't believe you.' And then he went on, reading in

Churchill as Prime Minister at work during a war-time train journey

silence. I was making a parallel with our Georges Clemenceau whom French people used to call 'the tiger'. Churchill gave me back my text. He had tears in his eyes. He simply said to me, 'It is much too kind of you.' He could not speak of my country's sufferings at that time without being deeply moved. It was astonishing to see the sensitive reactions cohabit in the same man with ruthless strength.

A little later when the German plane was flying over Downing Street, he burst out in loud imprecations: 'They will try to destroy this ancient city of ours but for one bomb that falls on London ten are going to fall on Berlin, for ten a hundred, for a hundred a thousand and for a thousand, thousands of thousands.' This apocalyptic eloquence sprang from the temperament of a man of war. In 1940 Churchill was fighting Hitler in single combat. 'They said he was a genius. He is not. He is the most monstrous abortion of human monstrosity.' The same evening when everything was ready for the broadcast, Churchill, dressed in a light blue siren-suit made of plush, was sitting comfortably in an armchair opposite innumerable microphones; there was no place for me to speak from. I asked 'Where can I sit, sir?' He looked round, saw nowhere to sit and, laughing, 'On my lap,' he said, throwing himself backwards. I put one of my legs between his, sat half on Churchill's thigh, half on his armchair's arm. The green light came on and the broadcast began.

Another glimpse of the mechanics behind those broadcasts which changed the destiny of men comes from one of his war-time secretaries, Mrs Elizabeth Nel:

Sometimes one would sit at the typewriter taking down his words straight into type, though as the war progressed and things were less strained, he came to prefer one to write in shorthand, which was easier. He would send everyone else from the room and would start pacing up and down, his forehead crinkled in thought, the cords of his dressing gown trailing behind him. He often wore his vivid red, green and gold dressing gown when dictating; it was a distinguished garment covered with dragons. Sometimes he would fling himself for a moment into a chair, sometimes pause to light his cigar which, with so much concentration, was neglected and frequently went out. For minutes he might walk up and down trying out sentences to himself. Then inspiration came, off he would go with tremendous fluency pacing round the room, his hands gesturing just as one knew they would be when he finally gave the speech and the long sentences came rolling out with all the force of his feelings.

Ed Murrow, who was in London reporting the Battle of Britain to America, remembers:

After an unusually severe night raid Mr Churchill was walking – I believe it was down the East India Dock Road, I can't be sure about this, and he was picking his way over the rubble and the street was filled with shattered glass and broken

With Mrs Churchill and Brendan Bracken (second from right) touring bomb damage in City of London, 1940

brick and the people came up out of the holes in the ground and cheered him to what is generally called the echo, and as the old man picked his way along, using his stick as an aid, the tears were running down his face and he said, 'They act as though I have brought them a great victory.' And I say he was crying with no sense of shame or embarrassment. If I had to write a caption for it I think I would say 'Too brave not to cry'.

Lord Mountbatten recalls a meeting which took place about two years later:

In October 1941 when I was in command of the aircraft carrier *Illustrious* the Prime Minister suddenly recalled me to London to report to him. His words made such an impression of unconquerable determination on me at that interview, that I remember the gist of them to this day: 'You will take over the command of Combined Operations from Admiral Keyes,' he said, 'you will continue commando raids as they are important to the morale of this country and our Allies, but your primary object will be to prepare for the great invasion. For unless we return to the Continent and beat the Germans on land we shall never win the war. All the other headquarters in this country,' he went on, 'are thinking defensively, your job will be to think only offensively. To restore the offensive spirit, to devise the technique, to create and develop the appliances and appurtenances as well as the assault ships and landing craft that will be needed. You will set up training centres where the three services will be trained as one. And you will organize the bases from which the great operation can be launched.'

Slowly, after many setbacks, and with many setbacks, the tide began to turn. By the end of 1941 Britain again had allies in the field, Russia and the United States.

General Lord Freyberg, V.C. recorded an impression of one of the Prime Minister's visits to the troops in Egypt in the course of one of his many journeys:

In World War II he took a personal interest in my command of the New Zealand expeditionary force, and he visited us on many occasions close to the front line in Egypt and in Italy. On one occasion he came on the eve of the Battle of Alamein, and had luncheon at my desert headquarters. Winston fascinated us by his accounts of what he had said to Stalin, and what Stalin had said to him. It appears that they were competing for the honour of which country had suffered most as a result of the war. Stalin was by no means getting everything his own way! Winston said: 'I don't agree that the Russian people are so badly off! Look at your box of matches – it is bigger than our British box and has more matches in it.' ('I knew that,' said Winston 'because I had already counted them!') 'And our box has only one striker while your Russian box has two.' Here a young subaltern intervened: 'I would not have said that to him, sir.' 'Why?' snapped Winston. 'Because Stalin might have said he wanted a Second Front.'

It was indeed a memorable occasion. We were still lunching and talking at 4 p.m. When we rose Winston said: 'Now I am going round your front line.' This I had to refuse because I could not allow him to go into the danger zone; he was angry and said so. He accused me of having taken him round the Somme battle-front in 1918 when he was Minister of Munitions, and yet in 1942 when he was Prime Minister and Minister of Defence I refused to let him visit this sector.

Taking leave of troops after visiting the 1st Army in Tunis area, 1943

I told him that had he been wounded in 1918 the general attitude would have been that it was a good show to get a Cabinet Minister involved in the battle, but in 1942 if I had risked one hair of Winston's head unnecessarily there would have been no forgiveness for me.

Winston Churchill will certainly be remembered as a diplomatist among his other claims to fame. What other man could have held the complex alliance together as he did? Mrs Roosevelt, reading from her book of memoirs,* tells something of the personal side in his official visits to the White House.

* *This I remember*, Hutchinson.

The friendship and affection between my husband and Mr Churchill grew with every visit, and was something quite apart from the official intercourse. It was evident that Great Britain and the United States would have to co-operate in any case, but the war could be carried on to better advantage with the two nations closely united through the personal friendship of Mr Churchill and my husband. The two men had many interests in common in addition to the paramount issue of the war. They were men who loved the sea and the Navy. They both knew a great deal of history and they had somewhat similar tastes in literature. It always gave my husband great joy when Mr Churchill quoted aptly from Lear's *Nonsense Rhymes* which were Franklin's favourites. Both of them had read much biography. My husband did not have the same interest in art, but both of them loved the out-of-doors and could enjoy themselves either in the country or the city. Their companionship grew, I think, with their respect for each other's ability. They did not agree on all things; I heard my husband make remarks which were sometimes inspired by annoyance and occasionally by a realistic facing of facts. I remember very well his irritation at Mr Churchill's determination that we should attack through Greece and the Balkans. Franklin said that would mean the loss of many men, though strategically it might be a help to Great Britain and might get us to Berlin before the Russians. However, he did not think that was important and he was not going to risk so many men. But I also remember the day Tobruk fell. Mr Churchill was with us when the news came, and though he was stricken, his immediate reaction was to say: 'Now what do we do?' To

His great personal friendship with Roosevelt: the two statesmen talking together in the conference room after the Yalta Conference in February 1945

neither of those men was there such a thing as not being able to meet a new situation. I never heard either of them say that ultimately we would not win the war. This attitude was contagious, and no one around either of them would ever have dared to say, 'I'm afraid'.

Most of the journeys were done by air. Group-Captain Mitchell has a personal recollection:

I was the navigator in the crew of Mr Churchill's personal aircraft from the spring of 1943 to the end of the war. The smooth operation on the domestic side gave the captain as many cares as did the flying of the aircraft itself. The provision of a menu which the P.M. enjoyed and the correct wines and spirits was not an easy matter overseas, and the risk of the P.M. being poisoned could not be overlooked. The aircraft was kept at Northolt, all in readiness should a direct summons take the captain and myself to No. 10 for a flight planning conference at which we would settle the routeing and timing of the journey. The question of flying risk with its attendant war-time dangers did not appear to trouble the P.M., but the tragic loss of Leslie Howard over the Bay of Biscay is a reminder that the enemy was ever after his life, and we took care never to fly the same route twice across those areas where we could have been intercepted by hostile patrols.

The P.M. was scrupulously fair in his dealings with his captain of aircraft and never attempted to override a firm decision as others had done with disastrous consequences; but woe betide the ifs and buts of a wavering reply to his questions. He seldom failed to spend some part of the journey on the flight deck, occupying either the co-pilot's seat or my own, demanding to be kept abreast of our progress and often commenting on his association with what passed below us. On one occasion he insisted on piloting the plane himself much to the astonishment of the fighter escort, Americans as it happened, and to the horror of his companions in the rear. Any gentle assistance from the captain was thrust aside as he insisted on trying to control it alone.

The invasion of the mainland of Europe, D-Day, approached. Field-Marshal Lord Montgomery has a curious memory of a conference:

On hearing how the invasion of Normandy was to be organized and carried out he came to the conclusion that too many vehicles were being landed on the beach and not enough soldiers, rifles, bayonets and tanks. He then said that he wished to come to my H.Q. which had then moved to the Portsmouth area, and discuss the problem with my staff. I decided that the best tactics would be to invite him to have dinner with me and my personal staff officers and he came on 19 May. When he arrived I asked him to come into my study for a private talk and he agreed. I then said to him 'I understand, sir, that you are not happy about the way in which the initial landings are to be made on the beaches and that you want to investigate the matter with my staff. I cannot allow you to do so. My staff do what I tell them. If you think something is wrong you can discuss it with me, not my staff. I consider the organization of the landing on the beaches is correct. If you disagree, it would mean you had no confidence in me.' I then looked at him and said 'Have you confidence in me?' There followed a somewhat awkward pause, after which he assured me he had absolute confidence in me and my troops. I then said, 'Now, sir, let's go next door and I will introduce you to my staff'. I did so, each in turn. When he reached the end of the line he turned and faced them and said, 'I wasn't allowed to talk to you people', and he smiled. Only a great man would have acted like that, and that's what he was, a very great man.

Robert Barr, at that time a BBC war correspondent, was at Portsmouth on 12 June 1944, when Mr Churchill joined the destroyer Kelvin *to sail to the Normandy beaches, and he remembers:*

With him was Sir Alan Brooke, Chief of the Imperial General Staff and Mr Churchill's old friend, Field-Marshal Smuts. We sailed for Normandy. From the moment we sailed Mr Churchill was on the bridge, it was a clear sunlit morning, and the Channel was busy with ships to-ing and fro-ing from Normandy to England. About halfway across we saw something that seemed to delight Mr Churchill; he was standing there on the bridge wearing a peaked blue sailor's cap, a reefer jacket and his binoculars slung round his neck, and ahead of us, as we watched, were the great caissons for Mulberry harbour being towed then over to the beach-head. One of them was particularly large, a great concrete cube about the size of a cinema, and it was very rough and ready still and sticking from the top were the umbrella heads of the reinforcements. He watched it through his binoculars for some time, seemed delighted, handed the binoculars to Smuts, and said: 'It reminds me of the Athenaeum'.

We crossed to Normandy and arrived at Sword Beach and there Mr Churchill, Sir Alan Brooke and Field-Marshal Smuts had lunch with General Montgomery. In the afternoon we toured the whole of the British beach-head from Arromanches to Ouistreham, sailing inshore and very slowly, Mr Churchill inspecting the beaches all the way along with his binoculars and as we reached Ouistreham, we continued to sail. We were sailing past the head of the British beach-head and the buzz went round that we were about to fire on the enemy. Gun crews were alerted, guns were loaded and we still sailed slowly on, past the beach-head, along the coast of enemy territory, and then it happened, something that caused a furore in the House of Commons next morning, for Mr Churchill leaned up over from the bridge and shouted 'fire'.

The guns fired on some unknown target, they fired again and again, and then *Kelvin* turned smartly to port and raced away from the German beaches. She had too valuable cargo on board. As we headed back down in the wardroom Mr Churchill was talking about counter-battery fire, as he said 'the moment in battle when dog eats dog', and over in a quiet corner Field-Marshal Smuts was talking to a midshipman, talking about the beauty of stained-glass windows.

In 1944 came the liberation of France. The end was now in sight.

Michel St Denis, remembers the Prime Minister's visit to Paris:

On 11 November 1944 I was a few yards behind Churchill on the Avenue des Champs Elysées, where side by side with General de Gaulle he was watching the march-past of the repatriated French forces. That day the Allied victory was,

Walking with General de Gaulle down the Champs Elysées to take the salute at a march-past following the liberation of Paris in August 1944

On the destroyer H.M.S. Kelvin when he crossed the Channel in June 1944 and inspected the beach-heads after the invasion of Normandy

above all, the victory of stubborn and faithful England. Liberation, independence and sovereignty recovered, were, for the common people of France, personified in the shape of this son of Marlborough, whom they could understand, admire and love. Winston Churchill is the first English hero to have entered France as a friend and as a liberator. This cannot be wiped out from French history.

It is easy to forget that while the last phase of the onslaught against Hitler's Reich took its eleven-month course Winston Churchill had not only to maintain his position as Britain's war leader but keep in a state of working efficiency a never wholly easy political coalition, and to preside over Commonwealth developments with which he was not always in complete sympathy. Lord Attlee was Deputy Prime Minister:

I was his deputy when he was abroad and often on occasions too I had suddenly to take on some job. I remember well how often at question time in the House of Commons, I wondered whether he was going to take questions. At the last moment perhaps I would be rung up and asked whether I would take questions; that was an awkward one because his replies to questions from backbench Tories were not always those that come well from a Labour Minister. I had hurriedly to re-form them.

I recall too towards the end of our period of the war, we were engaged, a great many of us, in preparing for the post-war period. We had committees of all parties and we agreed really wonderfully. Sir Winston was always rather suspicious when we agreed. He had an idea that the subtle Socialists were pulling the wool over the eyes of the innocent Tories. He always liked to get some outside opinion: might be Lord Cherwell, the Prof., might be Brendan Bracken. When the matter came up all the objections we had already dealt with in committee used to be trotted out; that was a bit tedious. But, on the whole, I suppose there was never a coalition government that worked with less friction than ours.

I think all of us, although sometimes irritated, had a great affection for Sir Winston Churchill. He was really a very lovable character. Even his little differences never made any difference. I had differences with him myself on occasions. I can remember an evening, when we were at it hammer-and-tongs for more than an hour over India, we used quite strong language: we were quite good friends the next day. Sir Winston never bore malice. A good man to work with; he made you work. But, above all, he loved the House of Commons. How often we have heard him say 'We refresh ourselves in the support of the House of Commons'. A great House of Commons man, a great democrat in a way. Though in his make-up he was a curious mixture. I sometimes compared him to one of those layer cakes, a layer of seventeenth century, a layer of eighteenth century, a layer of nineteenth century: possibly even a layer of twentieth. Altogether one must say that he was the most protean person I ever came into contact with.

Winston Churchill found himself out of office but not in the political wilderness; he was now the Leader of the Opposition. His position in Britain and Europe was unique and he led almost as crowded a public life as he had done as Prime Minister. He returned to office in 1951. But for the moment remember again the private life, and let not the image of the great warrior and leader and statesman make us forget the side of him that people imitated in friendly parody, or made crowds shout 'Good old Winnie!' The post-war years were again ones of intense literary output. Alan Hodge was his research assistant when he was writing his History of the English-Speaking Peoples.

I was asked to meet him at Chartwell with the idea of becoming his assistant in history. With his exquisite courtesy, and irresistible air of command, he spread his finely tapered fingers upon the luncheon table and invited my company and that of scholars I might recommend to 'browse in these extensive pastures': by this he meant the entire range of British, American and Commonwealth history from Roman times until the beginning of the twentieth century. Shortly afterwards he wrote to me, defining his aim. This is what he said: 'In this story we are keeping alive the famous dramatic incidents and not hesitating to produce cameos of detail when they are worth it. We are recording the march of events in what is meant to be a lively continuous narrative. Chronology is the secret of narrative. We are primarily concerned with the social and political changes which occur, especially with those which have left their marks on Britain and the United States today. All this was in my mind,' he wrote, 'when I collected the material and tried to tell the story. The theme is *A History of the English-Speaking Peoples* as viewed by the modern eye.'

There then began a time of immense activity for a number of expert historical advisers all over the country, as well as for myself. Sir Winston had a formidable range of historical imagination and knowledge, and an almost infinite capacity for important or picturesque detail. On some themes he had fixed ideas – the parsimony of the first Queen Elizabeth, for example, or the tyrannical brutality of Henry VIII. 'Six wives,' he said once, 'and look what he did to them.' But he would always listen to the experts.

His assistants were kept busy by the fertility of his enquiries. It might be on some large matter, such as the development of Common Law, or the destiny of the Napoleonic Empire. Or it might be on something small – a cameo, as he called it, vital to his presentation. For instance, he asked me to find out the exact wording of the first recorded story of King Alfred and the incident with the cakes.

My favourite memory is of going to 10 Downing Street not long before his retirement and finding the Private Secretaries' room full of dispatch boxes arriving, and ringing with incessant telephones. The baize door into the Cabinet room was shut, and orders had been given that it was not to be opened until 6.30, when I was to be shown in. Sir Winston was sitting alone at the long Cabinet Table. He had chosen to take twenty minutes relaxation from public business. He was re-reading Scott's novel, *Quentin Durward*. As I approached, he pushed it aside, saying, 'That is a good book. Now, what have you brought me?' And so we immediately got down to historical essentials.

Partly American himself, Winston Churchill's closest concern was to draw his own country and all Europe, and the British Commonwealth into practical relationship with the United States of America, and it is fitting that the last of these memories should be that of an American, Mr Lewis Douglas. He recalls the occasion when

Winston Churchill visited him soon after Mr Douglas had had the misfortune to lose an eye through a fishing accident.

I shall never forget when he called upon me after I had demonstrated my accuracy as a fly fisherman. I recall so clearly his sitting by my side and very gently placing his hand on my knee and saying in that extraordinary voice of his 'My dear Lew, you must not let this bother you, you must remember, you must remember, Nelson had only one eye'.

Sir Winston: a study by Cecil Beaton, 1943

Memories of Sir Winston Churchill

In this programme RICHARD DIMBLEBY introduced and
questioned five people, LADY VIOLET BONHAM CARTER
(BARONESS ASQUITH), ALAN BULLOCK, SIR IAN JACOB,
SIR RICHARD PIM and LORD MORRISON OF LAMBETH,
who knew Churchill

*An edited version
of the 'Panorama'
programme broadcast
in BBC Television
25 January 1965*

LADY ASQUITH: I was nineteen when I first met him. It is true that he's been
my dear and lifelong friend – a friend of friends – whose existence gave my life a
new dimension. Apart from loving him, to share his thoughts, to watch the workings of his extraordinary mind was a never-ending adventure. But I think that from
the moment of our first meeting, in my early youth, I saw him always in a kind of
dual perspective. Through and beyond my friend, well known and dearly loved,
I've always seen one of the greatest figures of all time, on the stage of history.

RICHARD DIMBLEBY: Where and when did you first meet him?

LADY ASQUITH: I first met him at a dinner party. He was then holding his first
government office, as Under-Secretary to the Colonies, in Sir Henry Campbell-
Bannerman's government. I found myself sitting next to this young man, who
seemed to me quite different from any other young man who'd ever come my way
before. And by a miracle we made immediate contact. Throughout the evening, I
listened to him spellbound. I remember thinking 'This is what people mean when
they talk of seeing stars. That's what I'm doing now'. When I got home, I rushed
upstairs, burst into my father's bedroom – where he always sat up reading for about
two hours before he went to bed – and told him: 'For the first time in my life I've
seen genius'.

RICHARD DIMBLEBY: What did your father say to that?

LADY ASQUITH: Well, he was sympathetic; he was very sympathetic, he said
that Winston was most remarkable, in many ways unique. He warned me then
and he proved quite right, that I shouldn't find many other people who agreed
with me.

RICHARD DIMBLEBY: Why do you suppose that, as the genius that you saw in
him, he was so rejected by so many people, and in fact for so long?

LADY ASQUITH: I marvelled then and I marvel now, at the length of time it
took his fellow countrymen and contemporaries to apprehend his greatness. I

suppose perhaps that he was too extraordinary to know how ordinary people work. And I think also that ordinary people like seeing in their statesmen a rather sublimated version of themselves. Sir Winston never could have been a version, sublimated or otherwise, of anyone else. But I think one political reason why he was for so long out of step with his contemporaries, is that he so often saw so much farther ahead than they did: for instance, his warnings of Nazi danger in the thirties – his appeal at Fulton to the free world to stand together in unity and strength, and again his Zürich speech, appealing to Europe to forgive old wrongs, and to unite and save itself – all these great flashes of prophetic vision were at the time either denounced, derided or ignored. Yet every single one of them has been vindicated by events.

RICHARD DIMBLEBY: The 1930's that you mentioned just then must have been a particularly frustrating time for him, surely?

On the steps of the ruined Chancellery, Berlin, 1945 (during a tour of the city when he attended the Potsdam Conference, July 1945)

LADY ASQUITH: He was in the shadows, he was at odds with his own party and with all the powers that be. Most people seemed asleep, and some shut their eyes deliberately. He devoted – he dedicated – all his powers of vision, passion and expression, to wakening the conscience of the nation, not only to its danger, but to its honour. And he failed. Awakening came only from the realization and fulfilment of the doom he'd prophesied, namely the Second World War.

RICHARD DIMBLEBY: But what was it in him that enabled him to switch from those years of frustration and of warnings, suddenly to become a leader in the forties whom everybody was willing to follow?

LADY ASQUITH: Well, I think it was mainly by being himself. He created in each one of us his own heroic vision of ourselves so that we were transmuted by his faith into the people who believed him. We were that people but we didn't know it until he had revealed us to ourselves.

RICHARD DIMBLEBY: Looking back over his great life what would you say are his really outstanding characteristics?

LADY ASQUITH: I should put courage first. The courage that accepts and hurls back every challenge – courage which he himself put highest among human qualities. Because, as he once said to me, 'it guarantees all the rest'. And then I think greatness of heart, what some people call magnanimity. He never sought to trample on a fallen foe, whether it was a political opponent or whether it was a defeated nation. Though he believed and he once said that 'there's only one answer to defeat, and that is victory', his enmity couldn't survive when victory was won. 'My hate had died with their surrender', he said, amid the ruins of Berlin. He never hated nations, or men as such. He only hated their ideas.

RICHARD DIMBLEBY: And any other quality would you see in him?

LADY ASQUITH: Vitality of course. He seemed to be endowed by nature not merely with a double charge of life, but with a double dose of human nature. And then, above all, transcending all the rest, his humanity. He was never a superman, he was a man; he was the most human of all human beings.

RICHARD DIMBLEBY: In those years when Churchill was out of office, he turned again and again to his work as an author. I suppose most of us ordinary folk will think about him always as a historian. What sort of historian was he? Alan Bullock, Master of St. Catherines College, Oxford, tells us:

ALAN BULLOCK: I think the word historian with its suggestion of a scholarly, critical, dispassionate observer, seems the strangest of words to apply to that passionate character, Sir Winston Churchill. It would be better to say that he was a great man of action, who turned to the writing of history as another form of self expression, almost as another form of action.

If you look at his books most of them are personal, in the sense that they are about the events in which he himself took part – *The River War*, *My Early Life*, his history of the First World War and its politics (*The World Crisis*), and then of course the six volumes on the Second World War. Even if you take the two famous biographies he wrote, they are in a curious sense personal, since one is a vindication of his father's career, in the *Life of Lord Randolph Churchill,* and the other a vindication of his great ancestor's career, his *Life of the Duke of Marlborough.*

There was about all his writing this extraordinarily attractive personal quality. And I think his view of history is exactly what you would expect of a great man of action. It is a heroic, dramatic view. He had a passion for great themes, and for great issues. If you take the great issues that were involved in the Second World War, the ordinary academic historian coming to it would refine, would show one within another, would make it more complicated; whereas Sir Winston, with the instinct of a man of action, makes it more simple. I cannot forbear to quote the theme, as he calls it, of his first volume of the *History of the Second World War:* 'How the English-speaking peoples, through their own wisdom, carelessness, and good nature, allowed the wicked to rearm'. And then the theme of the last volume: 'How the great democracies triumphed, and so were able to resume the follies which had so nearly cost them their lives'.

There is all, to me, of Churchill as a historian in those two magnificent phrases, seeing the issues in bold primary colours, simple issues between truth and falsehood, between right and wrong, between loyalty and treachery, not because he was a man without a subtle mind – this he had – but because his instinct as a man of action was to reduce the subtleties to simple, straightforward issues which could be decided this way or that.

What attracted him in history was what attracted him in action: conflict and

Working in his study at Chartwell (1930's)

crisis, in politics and in war. When the tides ran high, this was the moment for the daring pilot in extremity. And he brought to the writing of history a knowledge, an almost unequalled knowledge, of these things – of what it felt like to be in a moment of great crisis, not seen from the outside but from inside; of what life was like when you were confronted with great decisions and had to make them. And this was to bring something to history that no one will ever learn from the study of documents. His style matched this. A style that was highflown, full-bodied, full of echoes of Gibbon and Dr Johnson. An orator's style with its love of a rolling period, of the set piece, of the vivid phrase. Again can you imagine any other historian beginning his work in this way? At the beginning of *The Second World War*, before you get the theme you get the Moral of the Work: 'In War, Resolution; in Defeat, Defiance; in Victory, Magnanimity; in Peace, Good will'.

Yet it was always a personal style. You think he is going to build it up and up as an orator does, and then he will suddenly throw away a sentence. Here is another passage from *The Second World War*. He has been talking about the position of Prime Minister, and he says that it is unique: 'If he trips he must be sustained; if he makes mistakes, they must be covered; if he sleeps, he must not be wantonly disturbed; if he is no good, he must be pole-axed'. That last phrase is a marvellous throw away which gives a sudden and unexpected twist to the whole sentence.

If you want to talk about his writing of history you have to see it always as the writing of a man who turned to history with all the interests, instincts, and experience of a great man of action. But it is a two-way traffic; in his actions you also see this love of history, this fascination with it, this deep sense of the past, this feeling for the movement of history, and of his own place in it, you see this affecting his actions.

When I met him between Munich and Dunkirk he was like a great actor who had not yet found his true role; like a great actor who was to play King Lear and cannot find it, he was a caged lion frustrated. The great opportunity in which at last all these superb qualities were brought out came in May 1940, and I think one of the reasons why he was able to take this opportunity so superbly, was because of his sense of the moment in history, of the historical occasion, and of his own role in it. This gave him a vision of what he could do. Perhaps if one may take lesser mortals you can say one constantly comes across occasions when you feel you could have done better if only you had realized in advance how great a moment this was going to be. Sir Winston did know in advance, he sensed it coming.

I can say this because one of the few times I met him was in February 1940, at the moment when the war seemed to be a stalemate. The phoney war it was called. He asked me to go and see him in Admiralty House. He wanted to talk about *A History of the English-Speaking Peoples*, the book that he was still trying to get finished. I had been helping him a little with it. He began to talk to me, and very soon, I think, forgot I was there, in the First Lord's Room, which is, you know, exactly the right setting. One night in February 1940, I remember there

54

was snow in the courtyard as I went in. And characteristically he said to the Duty Officer: 'I am not to be disturbed unless the German High Seas Fleet is brought to battle'. He ushered me into the First Lord's Room and he talked for something like two hours about how he saw the history of his lifetime. And I sat there almost bewildered by the power this man displayed as he talked, how he saw the whole history of this country in his lifetime rising to a climax, the climax of what he called 'a death grapple with Germany'. He felt in advance the crisis that was coming, and with the same sense of frustration which he had had in the nineteen-thirties when he could not persuade people in this country, could not make them realize how tremendous, how grave, was the issue. I could see that if he were right about this, here was a man who had the historical imagination to grasp how the whole history of this country was coming to a climax. At that moment he could see not only the historic occasion but himself, I think, in the historic role.

When the moment came it was because of this deep feeling for history and his part in it that he was able to draw upon such reserves of strength to meet the crisis. So I think that Sir Winston's writing of history was not something apart, a relaxation, a diversion – perhaps like his painting – it was central to him, central to his way of looking at the world. He saw it all in terms of this great historical perspective. There has only been one other man in my lifetime who had this same feeling for the past, and who has drawn from it something of this same superb confidence as Sir Winston, and this is General de Gaulle.

I believe therefore that you must put the two sides together – the man of action writing history, and the student of history expressing his historical imagination, not only in writing but in action. It was fortunate for us that he not only had imagination to see this but could find in history an inexhaustible source of strength with which to rise to so great an occasion.

I think ours is an anti-heroic age. It is an age in which perhaps since the First World War heroism has not been at a discount but it has been suspect. Our mood in face of doubts and anxieties and perplexities and frustration is really to run for cover, not to expose oneself. The great heroic gestures, the great heroic words, the great heroic characters of, say, the nineteenth century, of the age of Garibaldi and so on, these are out of key and out of touch with our age as we know it. And Sir Winston completely defied this. In the midst of all this, here was a man cast in the heroic mould who loved the heroic gesture and spoke and rode into action with total confidence, exposing himself completely, if you like. He never took cover at all. His courage, his nobility – this I think is what fascinated us. It is not only that he himself lived life so fully and so magnificently and with these splendid gestures, with this magnanimity and courage, it is also that secretly we all feel this is the way life should be lived. For this reason he has fastened on our imaginations.

RICHARD DIMBLEBY: Here are two men who were close to Churchill in an intimate and often homely way: Sir Ian Jacob, who was the Assistant Military Secretary of the War Cabinet, under Winston Churchill, and Sir Richard Pim, Captain and one of the only eight Captains of the Royal Naval Volunteer Reserve, at that time, who was appointed to take charge of Churchill's Map Room, and went with him wherever he went throughout the whole of the war. Sir Ian, you were there, on the spot, at the moment when Churchill was appointed Prime Minister, and took over direction of the war at a desperate moment. What was the impact on everybody round him and on people farther afield when this happened?

Sir Ian Jacob: It was immediate and quite remarkable – we had been a little bit worried when we heard that he was to be Prime Minister; he was a man obviously of tremendous quality and strength, but apparently disorganized, and we wondered what would happen. Then suddenly we felt his drive and here, for the first time I suppose, since perhaps the days of Pitt, the conduct of a war by this country found itself in the grip of a man who really knew what he was doing. And it was fortunate also that he had, ready to be harnessed to do, and to carry out what he wanted to do, the best military machine that we had ever had, through the Chiefs of Staff and their subordinate organs. The situation was desperate, France was being overrun, and any lesser man would have been over-whelmed, I think.

Richard Dimbleby: What were the attributes that you could see in him that made him instantly – apart from being such a leader – such a tower of strength to everybody else?

Sir Ian Jacob: First of all, as Lady Asquith has said, courage – mental and physical – he was entirely unmoved by whatever happened. He was equally unmoved by success or failure. Secondly, there was a sense that he knew what was going on, that he knew what should be done and that his great historical grasp of the situation meant that he understood all the forces at work and knew how to cope with them. Then, I think, the other extraordinary characteristic was his thoroughness. Whenever he set to work on something he carried it right through. I've never yet heard him say: 'Well that's enough for this evening, we'll go on with this tomorrow morning'. It had to be finished, and thoroughly finished.

Richard Dimbleby: One gets the impression, when you read his books of the war period, that he was always dealing with a multitude of things at once. Had he, in fact, the power to do this or did he like to do one thing at a time to the end and then turn to the next?

Sir Ian Jacob: Well, he had this extraordinary wide grasp but, nevertheless, he was really happy when he was concentrating on something. He got almost cantankerous when nothing in particular was happening; what he really liked to do was to find that there was some great project in front of him which he could concentrate on and drive through and make quite certain that it was going to be a success. He didn't like the steady flow of events.

Richard Dimbleby: Is it true that he carried out these prodigies of work that everybody talks about – you were a member of his very close staff – did he in fact work everyone to death?

Sir Ian Jacob: He very nearly did. He kept himself going, of course, by his afternoon sleep – he could go to sleep instantly. The moment he went to bed he went to sleep but he had only one hour, or an hour-and-a-half's sleep every after-noon, and then he was fit and on the top line until three a.m. But I think that he was able to do this tremendous work because he had a constitution which was quite unusual – I've always thought that somebody ought to study his constitution. How a man could do what he did, day in, day out for six years, at that age is absolutely extraordinary.

RICHARD DIMBLEBY: Supposing that he had been asked, what do you think he would have thought was his greatest success in the war? What would he have thought was his greatest failure, if there was one?

SIR IAN JACOB: I think his greatest success was due to his grasp, right at the beginning, that nothing mattered except the United States and he set to work to get alongside the President from the moment war was declared and he did succeed in that – in getting that wonderful harmony between the British and the American effort without which, I think, the war could hardly have been won. His failure, if you can call it a failure, was that he couldn't convince either the Americans, or anybody else, of the terrible results which would flow from the admission, as it were, of the Russians into the centre of Europe.

RICHARD DIMBLEBY: Sir Richard Pim, what exactly was your job in charge of the Map Room?

SIR RICHARD PIM: The main duty was to keep a pictorial record of the war at sea, on land and in the air, brought up to date every four hours for the whole six years of the war. And, when we were abroad, to bring with us maps and from such signals as were received wherever we were, to plot those signals and show Sir Winston the position. It was a very personal relationship because we were always close to him, either below his bedroom; or, if we were away out of Great Britain, we were usually next to his bedroom, so that he could come in and out whenever he wished.

RICHARD DIMBLEBY: How much, in fact, did you see of him day by day, night by night?

SIR RICHARD PIM: I went in at eight o'clock in the morning with his breakfast and told him what had happened during the night and then he would come in and out during the day as he had time and we would see him again immediately after his sleep in the evening and then, quite likely, there would be a meeting of the Chiefs of Staff in the Map Room going on perhaps until two in the morning, as Sir Ian has just remarked. Then, before he went to bed, he always came in to see the last picture.

RICHARD DIMBLEBY: I remember a quotation from Churchill – 'the Prime Minister is never wantonly to be disturbed'. Did you ever have to do this?

SIR RICHARD PIM: Only once. That was on the occasion that the Germans invaded Greece and I, with great trepidation, woke him up at about five in the morning, thinking this was of great importance to him and he listened. The only remark he made was: 'I am not to be awakened again unless Britain is invaded'. He never was.

Close-up of a section of one of the wall maps in the underground H.Q., showing positions of naval convoys

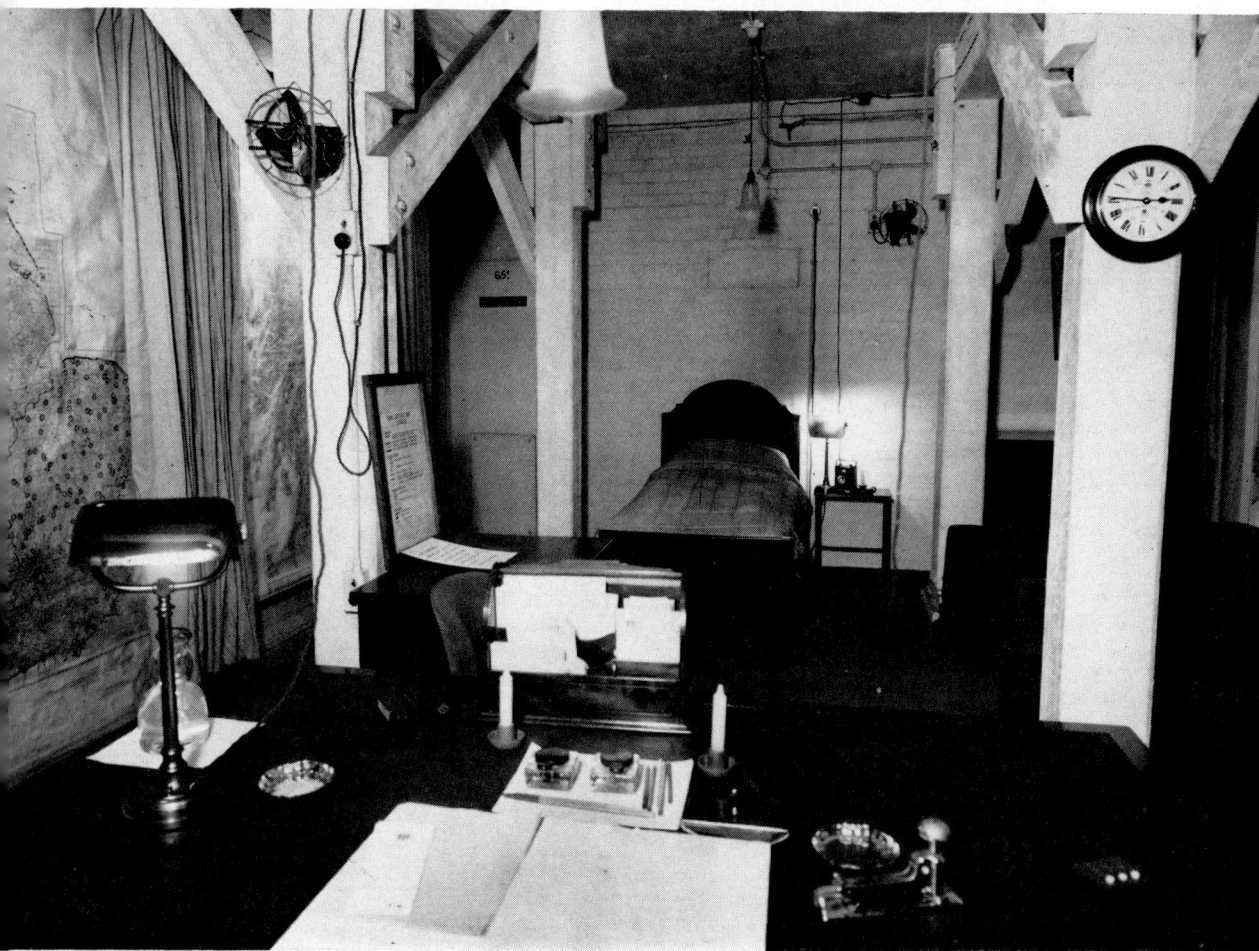

Churchill's combined bedroom and office which he used during the war at the underground H.Q. in London of the War Cabinet and Chiefs of Staff

RICHARD DIMBLEBY: Obviously he was a difficult person to work for, because he demanded such an enormous amount from the people around him. But he was not an impossible, or in any way an unpleasant person to work for?

SIR RICHARD PIM: Oh dear, no. Very much the reverse. He was, and I say it with absolute conviction, held in deep affection. One of the reasons was that if any of his staff were ill, or out of sorts, he would go to any trouble to find out what he could do for them. He enjoyed doctoring them too, that was something he enjoyed.

RICHARD DIMBLEBY: And giving them often the wrong pills I am told?

SIR RICHARD PIM: Well, that one wouldn't know. I don't think the pills did us any harm. But he was full of sympathy, not only for his staff, but for the unfortunate people who were wounded or casualties in air raids or at sea, or wherever it might be. And his grief was very real. He told me on many occasions that he didn't think the Anglo-Saxon liked showing any sentiment. He personally was different to that.

On one occasion, three destroyers – I think it was off Narvik – were sunk and, when I told him this at breakfast-time, the tears trickled down his cheek and then his whole mood changed at once and he said: 'Always remember that if they've done that to us, what must we have done to them? The British fleet always reports its casualties first'. He was so completely full of confidence in the forces and what they were doing. And he did, of course, go in for a considerable amount of detail. One had to carry it in one's head. I do remember at two o'clock in the morning when he was going up to bed, I had told him about a ship being sunk, which he'd been interested in, and he asked me what the cargo was. I told him it had many tons of eggs from America for Great Britain, and he said: 'Ah Pim, how many eggs are there in a ton?' That I couldn't answer, but I told him I'd find out by ringing up the Minister concerned. And he said: 'Yes, you do that'. And he sat down beside me by the telephone. I rang the Minister concerned and I asked him to let me know how many eggs there were in a ton. I've always felt since that Minister must in all probability have thought a lunatic was talking to him, but I explained what it was all about and, by about four or five o'clock in the morning, I got the answer. Sir Winston wanted it for an early meeting of the House, and he considered this of great importance in a discussion on the food situation in Great Britain. This was just one example of the kind of detail he might require.

RICHARD DIMBLEBY: Do you have any particularly vivid personal memories of him?

SIR RICHARD PIM: One was in Quebec where I went into his room in the early morning at the same time as his breakfast, and there he was dropping eye lotion into his butler's eye. I had to hold the butler's head and he was acting as doctor. That was a wonderful picture of the Prime Minister. Another I will always remember is on the voyage from Newfoundland, on board the battleship

Prince of Wales to Iceland. He'd been told to stay in bed. He had a very bad cough that day and, when I went in to tell him we were coming up on a convoy to England, he was smoking a cigar: when I asked him why, he said: 'Well, what the eye doesn't see the heart doesn't grieve over and the doctor is at the other end of the ship'. He insisted on coming up on the bridge and waving to the convoy as he went through, and that is a picture I, and I'm sure the men in that convoy, will always remember. Lastly, at the end of the war, the day of the election, we came back from Potsdam in the summer of 1945, and the first results of the poll came through while Sir Winston was in his bath. I went in and I read out the first ten or twelve results which were very much against his Party. He thought for a moment and then he said: 'This may well be a landslide and they have a perfect right to kick us out. That is democracy. That is what we've been fighting for; hand me my towel.' That evening he asked me to get his car to go to the Palace and I did that, and just as he was going off to the Palace he came in, and this is purely a personal memory, and he said: 'Pim, here are two bottles of champagne. You will now be going back to Ulster. Thank you and God bless you.' And that I can never forget.

RICHARD DIMBLEBY: Lord Morrison, how do you think of him as a parliamentarian?

LORD MORRISON: He was a great parliamentarian there's no doubt. Mind you, he was not altogether familiar always with the procedure of the House or the Standing Orders but that's not uncommon. And another point I noticed was that he wasn't anxious to take part in the immediate cut and thrust of debate, that is to say – to jump in after another Member had spoken and go for him and undo his arguments. He preferred the speech that was carefully prepared and then would be brilliantly delivered. When his name went up on the ticker or Mr Lloyd George's name went up on the ticker the House immediately filled. The House loved listening to these two great orators and parliamentarians at that period. But the curious thing was that neither of them nor their arguments altered, I think, by a single vote the decision of the House. Lloyd George was in the Liberal Party and therefore the Conservatives had no particular room for him. Winston had been a naughty boy from the Conservative point of view and had been a nuisance to them and was out in the wilderness as Lady Asquith has described to us. And so there was a prejudice against both of them but a passionate wish to listen to both of them as first-class parliamentary orators.

The other time I remember Winston as a parliamentarian was when he was Leader of the Opposition and I was Leader of the House of Commons in the Labour Government. He attacked us with great violence and vigour but, I think, without malice. On Thursday afternoons I had to announce the business of the House for the following week, and he used to have fun and games and attack me and the Government too. In fact this became known later as the Children's Hour and when I heard of this I said to Winston – 'Winston, we ought to drop this fun and games on Thursday afternoons. They're beginning to talk about the Children's

Hour'. He listened and in about a fortnight he did drop it and gave the job to Anthony Eden, though it didn't stop him jumping in when he wanted to.

One day he must have delivered about a column and a half of Hansard of first-class abuse of me. It really was abusive and insulting stuff. And it was so well done that I sat there and thoroughly enjoyed it; at the end he sat down, I answered, and then he put his head beside the dispatch-box, gave me a great big wink as much as to say – 'Herbert, no offence, it's all part of the game'.

Without question he was the one man to be the war-time Prime Minister. There can be no question about that whatever. That isn't to say that he was perfect, as none of us are, and he wouldn't claim to have been. But as war leader he did a job that maybe somebody else could have done but I can't imagine anybody in public life at that time who could have done the job with the ability and the spirit that he did. He was the leader of the nation in the true sense of the term.

He shared his disappointments, setbacks, and the country's defeats with the nation. He would set aside two or three days in almost isolation to prepare those parliamentary speeches or broadcast addresses telling the nation about the progress, or the non-progress, of the war. And this must be said to his great credit: he never tried to deceive the country into believing that we were doing better than we were doing. In fact, one of his great parliamentary phrases that I remember – I think it was after our defeat in Singapore – was: 'Mr Speaker, I come to report bad news for the House and the country and, Mr Speaker, there is worse to come'.

That addition of the 'worse to come' was a stroke of genius and a stroke of honesty because it prepared the country for more trouble and the British are of a character that if you are frank with them they will tighten things up, they will – as Shakespeare said in one of the Henry plays* – what is it? 'Now set the teeth and stretch the nostril wide.' Therefore Churchill's method paid. Not only was it right morally in itself and politically right but it was tactically right to admit to the nation that things were not going well and then to say, to give full measure, 'there is worse to come'. These, I think, were among the great things. And somebody may say – well, why did he waste all that time preparing those speeches? They were not a waste of time. They paid. They were good, not only for the morale of the country and for the morale of the forces but they were good for our friends abroad, and I think they struck a bit of terror into the hearts of Hitler and company.

RICHARD DIMBLEBY: I know that Churchill in 1945 blamed you largely as the architect of the Labour victory of that year and was put out, but basically none of this made any difference to your relationship and your real basic friendship with him did it?

LORD MORRISON: Not in the long run. It did for a little. I remember when I was going to meetings over London, apart from meetings of my own constituency, I passed him on his triumphal tour through south London three nights. A most curious thing, it was an accident, and there he was standing up in the car, long cigar smoked, as to which I felt a bit envious, and waving to the people and the

* *Henry V*, act III, scene i.

people cheering with very, very great ardour and enthusiasm. And if ever a man was entitled to believe that he was winning that election, Winston was. But the fact was that the British had reached a stage of life in which they were thinking more for themselves and about the situation than they had ever done electorally before. It so happened that they cheered Winston because they wanted to thank him as war-time Prime Minister, that they thought he was a good war-time Prime Minister but his party would not be a good peace-time government, and after the cheering most of them went away and voted against him.

If he was disappointed and even a bit bitter about that I can understand it but we have been told that bitterness didn't enter into it. But he was cross with me. There had been a little – not a little, a nasty – air raid incident in Lewisham before I was the candidate, and it arose out of a decision he had made that there should be no warnings unless there was more than one enemy aircraft over the country, and questions at my meetings compelled me to draw out that it was his decision.

Standing in the ruins of the Chamber of the House of Commons, 1940

He went to the meeting that night, his meeting at the Clock Tower, Lewisham, and he said: 'Of all my late colleagues, the one that I never want to see again is Herbert Morrison'. And I answered that night and he said he would and he might be on the Opposition benches and I might be on the government, and it so happened that that's what happened.

RICHARD DIMBLEBY: But this didn't last long, did it?

LORD MORRISON: No. For about three weeks he refused to talk to me and we had to go side by side to the House of Lords, because Attlee was away at Potsdam. He refused to talk to me. And one day I said – 'Well look, it's not far to the House of Lords is it?' and he said – 'Hm, hm, ugh – I do not wish to talk with you at all until you have answered a letter which I am about to send you', and that was about this bombing incident, you see. And so it was and I was very sorry about it, but I understood. Then I met him at No. 10 at a reception one night and I didn't go over to see him because I thought he might rebuff me as he had before and I didn't want to have any unpleasantness with him, but he beckoned me over and he then said: 'Herbert, I've never told you before but when you became Minister of Home Security and Home Secretary in the bombing, you performed one of the most courageous political acts of any politician I've ever known and I am very grateful to you for doing it'. And ever since then we've been buddies. My wife and I have been to Chartwell to lunch and we've had drinks together in the House of Commons and sometimes he's given me a cigar, sometimes large and sometimes small, according to how he was feeling.

RICHARD DIMBLEBY: What is your final memory of him?

LORD MORRISON: My final assessment is one of wonderment and a complimentary one. Here he is. He's led a great controversial life. He was in the General Strike with flying colours against the Trades Union Congress. He said that Labour wasn't fit to govern years and years ago. He has fought us. He's quarrelled with the Conservative Party about India and so on. He's been in the Liberal Party and out of the Liberal Party, in the Conservative Party and out of it and back again. So he's led a controversial life. Yet in his recent years he's achieved a position more unique, more exceptional, more great than any other politician of our time and I think in any other politician's time. He has become, so to speak, the darling of the nation, loved, admired and respected by everybody and his passing will produce from the eyes of many people – Conservative, Labour, Liberal – people of all political views and religions and none – it will produce tears for the loss of a very, very great man: Winston Churchill, the darling of the nation.

'The greatest man any of us have known'

by the Rt Hon. HAROLD WILSON, M.P., The Prime Minister

TONIGHT our nation pays its tribute to the greatest man any of us have known. *Broadcast* *24 January 1965* While the world shares in the sense of loss and pays tribute to Winston Churchill's life and achievements, we in Britain feel as a family feels, when its eldest, most respected, best-loved member dies: a sense of personal loss, of a gap in our midst that cannot be filled.

The silent vigil of our people outside his house for so many dark hours; the unstinted sympathy felt in every home in the land for Lady Churchill – these are perhaps more eloquent of our feelings than any words can be.

Parliament will tomorrow pay its united tribute to a great parliamentarian and a great statesman. Her Majesty the Queen has expressed the will of the nation in her wish that Sir Winston be accorded a State funeral. The service in St Paul's Cathedral, where lie the heroes of an earlier war of Britain's survival, and the lying in state in Westminster Hall, the ancient heart of the Palace of Westminster, will provide the fitting surroundings for the honour that we as a nation pay his memory. But the deepest tribute, the deepest gratitude to him will be in our own hearts and minds.

We know, too, that with his death we are marking the end of an era. Winston Churchill's public life spans the memory of almost every one of us. Even before his entry into Parliament, sixty-five years ago, he was a well-known, even a controversial, figure. His thirst for adventure, his disregard of personal safety, which never left him, had taken him early into the Queen's service in the Fourth Hussars, into the prisoner-of-war compound, and then out of it. He charged with the Lancers at Omdurman, he was one of the first into Ladysmith.

From his election as Member of Parliament for Oldham at the age of twenty-five, his public life was no less tempestuous, from the Free Trade battle of his earliest years to the bitter controversies that surrounded military preparations and military policies of two world wars.

It is nearly sixty years since he first became a Minister of the Crown. And he has held practically every high office in the State. At the Board of Trade, over half a century ago, he was concerned with the first steps towards National Insurance and the social revolution of our times. As Father of the House he lived to see the Welfare State.

64

In the first war, he one minute carried the awesome responsibilities of First Lord of the Admiralty; in another he found himself a controversial, defeated ex-Minister, who sought a new duty in Flanders. Between the wars, he held the strings of Treasury power as Chancellor – a few years later he was an outcast, when he warned of the dangers that Britain faced as the shadow of the jack-boot menaced European civilization. And, in September 1939, when his forebodings were realized, every man serving in every ship, in the far-flung Royal Navy, already deployed in its war posture, was electrified by the three-word signal from the Board of Admiralty: 'Winston is back'.

But it was his leadership of that war-time team, that great united team – Ministers of all parties, commanders and fighting men, the men and women of ammunition factories and those who kept going the essential home services – each of them willing to submerge his own identity and interest in a great cause under his lead, it was that leadership and that response which saved Britain and saved freedom.

In his war memoirs he tells of his 'profound sense of relief' when in the midst of the disasters of the battle of France he became Prime Minister. 'I felt,' he said, 'as if I were walking with destiny, and that all my past life had been but a preparation for this hour and for this trial. . . . Therefore, although impatient for the morning, I slept soundly and had no need for cheering dreams.'

The morning, and all the mornings, provided the proof. Those five years brought forth the qualities born in him, the qualities he had nurtured. First, the quality of indomitable courage. Never in the hour of greatest peril doubting ultimate victory, he could at once rebuke and inspire fainter hearts than his own. That inner certainty which enabled him to stand almost alone in seeing and warning of the danger, that certainty became an unshakeable rock when it was Britain and the Commonwealth who stood alone.

Second, his power to evoke an undeniable response. Winston Churchill had through his power over words, but still more through his power over the hearts of men, that rare ability to call out from those who heard him the sense that they were a necessary part of something greater than themselves; the ability to make each one feel just that much greater than he had been; the ability which runs like a golden thread through our national history to inspire a slumbering nation so that it can call up those inner reserves of effort and of character which have never failed us when our very survival has been at stake.

Thirdly, the quality of humanity. The man who could move armies and navies and embrace the world in one strategic sweep could himself be moved to uncontrollable and unashamed tears at the sight of an old soul's cheerfulness in a shelter or of a street of devastated houses, at the thought of the human realities which lay behind the war communiqués.

It was his courage, his humanity, the response he evoked in our people that wrote in those war-time years that imperishable chapter in our history, a chapter which will always bear the title he gave to one part of that chapter, 'Our finest hour'. Far overriding and sustaining those qualities which marked his years of leadership was his great sense of history, of, in his own words, 'walking with destiny' – thinking there not so much perhaps of himself but of his country and of the Commonwealth.

His power over the written and spoken word, which has illuminated his own historical writings, was itself thrown into clearer relief by his sense of making history and writing history, not as distinct occupations but as part of a wider whole; and it is because of this that the words and deeds of Winston Churchill will form part of the rich heritage of our nation and of our time for as long as history comes to be written and to be read.

Now, his pen and his sword are equally at rest. The tempestuous vitality of a man who would have scorned the ease of a peaceful retreat has ended today in quiet, in peace, in stillness. But what every one of us can know is that Winston Churchill's life, his monumental achievements, have enriched forever not only our nation which he led, not only the world which he bestrode, but the hearts of each of us whose lives he touched with his greatness.

Churchill speaking at an open-air meeting in Amsterdam when he attended The Hague Congress organized by the International Committee of the Movements for European Unity, 1948

Leader of resistance to tyranny

by the Rt Hon. SIR ALEC DOUGLAS-HOME, M.P., Leader of the
Conservative Party

*Broadcast
24 January 1965*

PERHAPS the greatest tribute which can be paid to Sir Winston Churchill is that
although by his deeds he earned all the superlatives, nevertheless when they are
applied to him they seem totally inadequate. The greatest of living Englishmen,
certainly, but that does not convey the vivid, compelling personality, controversial
and colourful, who commanded the centre of the political stage for something
like half a century in our country. The incomparable war leader, yes, but that does
not etch for us with sufficient clarity the picture which you and I knew so well
of the indomitable figure four-square on the cliffs of Dover or against the livid
London sky, defying evil and personifying the resistance of free people everywhere
to tyranny.

The finest orator, yes, but that cannot recapture for us the thrill of those words
which set the blood tingling through the veins of patriots and sent out ordinary
men and women to deeds of valour which were almost superhuman.

Sir Winston had, too, vision in a degree rarely given to a man; and his work
for the English-speaking peoples and for the unity of Europe will endure, and his
speeches on the theme of interdependence and of one world will, I am certain, be
looked upon by our children and grandchildren as prophetic.

He became, after a varied and a long political life, Leader of the Conservative
Party both as Prime Minister and in Opposition. And when I served under him I
never heard him think or say a mean thought or word. Indeed, he set himself only
one standard which he exacted from others, and that was unselfish service in the
service of the whole nation.

Personally he had an abundance of two of the greatest of qualities: the first,
humanity, and the second, loyalty. It was because ordinary men and women
sensed these things that they quite simply loved him. Perhaps he would allow us,
today, to make the sign which he made so much his own – the sign of victory – for
today Winston Churchill has won the battle and he has won it triumphantly.

I hope that Lady Churchill and his family will know that all of us in the nation
are trying our best to express at once our sorrow, our gratitude, and our understanding.

Always a controversial figure

by the Rt Hon. JO GRIMOND, M.P., Leader of the
Liberal Party

ALTHOUGH we may have realized that a life lived so vigorously for ninety years must be coming to its close, yet the death of Sir Winston Churchill and his passing into history not only stamp an epoch but come as a sense of deep shock and loss to us all.

*Broadcast
24 January 1965*

Much has been written on his exploits, and they will be retold and revalued by generation after generation. But what does the career of this man mean to us of this generation; why, in particular, do we salute him, this man whose life started in worlds so very different from our own?

First, we admire the romance of his life, its buccaneering quality, and particularly so because it differs so much in that respect from our own. We remember his adventures in Africa, and the very individual and indeed erratic course of his career in politics, unlike that of most politicians and probably impossible of repetition. A young Winston today setting out in politics would soon find himself driven out of the tight sheepfolds which are imposed now by the modern party system.

We like his pugnacity. He was always a controversial figure, and we refuse to have him overlaid with the cloying sweetness of universal and undiscriminating praise. He made many mistakes; he was much abused; he had to fight his own party in the days before the war when he felt that they were pursuing policies harmful to Britain. In fact, he seemed to have ended all hope of office or influence for the sake of what he believed to be right.

We admire his intellectual curiosity, and his intellectual vigour. He was never trivial. You only had to have the shortest conversation with him to realize that his mind was always ranging in a big way over big ideas. He was always playing with the future and its possibilities. We remember his constant probing for new roads to victory in both wars, and we remember, too, the way he goaded and directed and dominated and cross-examined his War Cabinet, and the very formidable experts who advised him. We admired his vigour and his will.

These are qualities which are essential to political life if politics is to be anything else except a sterile pursuit of office and a careful calculation of personal benefit; and no one of recent years has done more to raise the level of politics in this country than did Sir Winston Churchill. A tragedy it is that he was not able

68

in peace, as he had been able in war, to drive his government into the leadership of Europe, because he saw so clearly where modern trends lay and he was the one man who could put this country at the head of a great European movement.

We respond to his humanity – he was, of course, one of that great Liberal Cabinet which founded the welfare state. But his humanity was also of a personal sort. He certainly enjoyed power – that was plain to see; but great leader though he was he was never haughty, he was never remote; he might be overbearing, he might be unfair, but never mean or cynical. And he enjoyed also all the luxuries which we ourselves would like to enjoy. And this is what, I think, endeared him to so many people: they saw in him their ambitions and, indeed, their vices writ large. They liked his warmth and his generosity and the open display he gave of his anger and his pleasure. They liked the pleasure he took in life itself.

All over Britain, sympathy will go out to his family, and in particular to his wife, who supported him so nobly through all the ups and downs of an almost incredible career.

Speaking at the Lord Mayor's banquet in Guildhall after becoming Prime Minister again in 1951

A romantic and adventurous life

by the Rt Hon. HAROLD MACMILLAN

Broadcast
24 January 1965

WE KNEW that it must come, but all the same it is a terrible shock. Yet those who loved him best would not have wished it otherwise. Although Churchill, with characteristic courage, managed to take and to give something worth while, even in the last stages of his life, yet each time that I have seen him in recent months I have felt that he was waiting – waiting patiently, hopefully, manfully, for his release.

It is one of the compensations which many of us have experienced in our own families, that when a very old man dies we forget at once the weakness and physical incapacity of the last few years. Our mind goes back, not to the old man we have just lost, but to the splendid figure of virility and courage of the man we knew in his prime.

We all have our memories of him. Many will recall, above everything else, the wonderful war speeches which thrilled and roused the whole nation, and were heard with equal enthusiasm by many a clandestine listener awaiting the day of liberation. Others will have seen him touring the bombed areas, his deeply sensitive nature much moved, giving out both sympathy and consolation. The East End of London has not forgotten the cry that went round after a bad night: 'Here's Winnie'. Countless soldiers, sailors, airmen will remember the keen, almost boyish enthusiasm with which he seized every opportunity to see things for himself. The stories about him are legion. Even those which are rebuttable illustrate one or other side of his rich character. His very faults proved virtues; his obstinacy could be exhausting. But that was only one side of the medal; on the other was stamped 'undefeatable determination never to give in'.

Perhaps the most endearing thing about him, in private talks, in the Cabinet, in the House of Commons, was his puckish humour, his tremendous sense of fun, and the quick alternation between grave and gay.

Churchill's life is, in itself, a great romance. He excelled in many fields: soldier, author, statesman. It was a life of adventure and hazard, for he was never afraid to take risks or to put his fortune to the test. Yet throughout all the various aspects of his career one strain has been constant and unchangeable: his love of Britain, of the Empire; his pride in its glorious past, his confidence in its future.

70

Those of us who were his friends before the war – before the second war – are now very few, and even those who served under him in his war government are only a handful. The man that we remember was great in failure and defeat as in success and victory. In the concluding days of the last Parliament, the House of Commons by the unanimous desire of all its members paid him a unique tribute. On this occasion I referred to the phrases printed in each volume of his last great work, *The Second World War*. He called these the morals of this work. They run thus: 'In war, resolution; in defeat, defiance; in victory, magnanimity; in peace, goodwill'. These splendid words sum up his whole life, and stand forever as his memorial.

In the next few days we shall be hearing and reading, once again, of his great achievements. Today, we mourn the man, although we knew it must come soon. There can be none of us who did not feel a sense of personal loss when we heard that the greatest heart in England had ceased to beat.

The gun-carriage bearing the coffin of Sir Winston, drawn by a naval detachment, on its way to St Paul's Cathedral, 30 January 1965

'The Talisman of Free Men'

by LORD AVON

THIS is a time not only for national mourning but of mourning throughout the free world, because the man of whom we speak did not belong to us alone. He epitomized our nation's resistance to the powers of evil which would have subdued us. And so he was the talisman of free men everywhere.

Broadcast
24 January 1965

Out of all our eighteen years of constant work together, my mind goes back today to the period of the Second World War which he called 'our finest hour', and which was certainly his. It was a time when nothing was left to our country, and to the Dominions who stood with us, except to hold on; none could see the light at the end of the tunnel. Courage for some sudden act, maybe in the heat of battle, we all respect; there is the still rarer courage which can sustain repeated disappointments, unexpected failure, and shattering defeat. Churchill had that too, and he had need of it; not for an hour or a day, but for weeks and months and even years. Looking back now at the war, victory may seem to have been certain, but it wasn't always so. And when the news is bad and the prospect bleak, it can be lonely at the top.

I saw much of Sir Winston then, often many times a day, not only at official meetings, but in such periods of comparative relaxation as there were, at meals, and late into the night. I grew to love him.

There is a granite type that feels little, but if set upon the right course can hold it. Sir Winston was none of that. He felt deeply every blow of fortune, and every gleam of hope. 'What's the news?' or 'Any news?' was his constantly repeated first question to any new arrival, whether he was colleague or an official. Alert, eager, and questioning, as his temper was he could hold on through all tides and tempests. And he knew when to reject 'No' as an answer. The arguments against any positive course will always marshal themselves. His mind was always projected to the next move. In all this he was aided by an energy which was more than a zest for life, a really medieval constitution, health and vigour, carried Churchill through crises and long hours of work. He would have survived any strain in any age, though he loved best the present one.

His opinions were inevitably of his own generation, and some have criticized him for it. They were wrong. He was open-minded and comprehending as few men are in this twentieth century. He saw clearly and further than most, and he

72

spoke of what he saw fearlessly and without favour. He sensed danger for his country with the touch of the artist, and the knowledge of the historian. It was a fascination to work with him. It was to live with greatness.

Joseph Addison wrote these lines of Sir Winston's famous ancestor after the victory of Blenheim. I think that Sir Winston would like their association today:

> Unbounded courage and compassion joined,
> Tempering each other in the victor's mind,
> Alternately proclaim him good and great,
> And make the hero and the man complete.

Winston Churchill giving his V-sign during the war

Dynamic Leader

by LORD MOUNTBATTEN

NEVER did I find him depart in the smallest degree from the spirit of the offensive that sustained him, and he inspired us all through his example. He was a constant source of novel and invigorating ideas, though by no means all of these were practicable, and certainly not all of them could have been carried out simultaneously.

Broadcast 24 January 1965

He was unfailingly open-minded and sympathetic to unorthodox suggestions which had not yet been tried out, put up by others. The effect of this great man's mind on us was to make us all think and to clear our own minds, so that we could adopt the best of the courses which he suggested.

But at all times he was first and foremost a dynamic and inspiring leader. It is impossible to overestimate the part he played in leading us to victory, or the debt that we all owe him.

All of us who worked with him will miss him very much – no one more than I.

Stepping ashore on the east bank of the Rhine, March 1945

The Severest Test

by SIR ROBERT BRUCE LOCKHART,
Deputy Under-Secretary of State, Foreign Office
and Director General of Political Warfare Executive, 1941-1945

An extract from a general news talk, broadcast in the European Service of the BBC 24 January 1965

IN A LIFE crowded with triumphs – yes, and disappointments too – the Battle of Britain was, I think, the severest test of Churchill's nerve and courage. On what proved to be the last day of the battle he went to Stanmore, the headquarters of Fighter Command, and there, standing beside Air Marshal Park, he watched on the radar screen the British fighters going up to meet the German bombers. Attack followed attack, and still there seemed no end. At last Churchill turned to the Air Marshal. 'How many squadrons have you left?' he asked, and Park answered very quietly: 'Those on the screen are the last.' In silence the two men waited: five minutes, ten minutes, a quarter of an hour. No more enemy planes appeared. The Germans had had enough. And with tears in his eyes Churchill got into his car and drove away.

They were tears of relief. He had other tears – tears of sorrow and of anger when he walked through the bombed streets of the East End of London, for this strong man, so rock-like in determination, was deeply stirred by the sufferings of others. In those days all England was behind him. His portrait was in every house and cottage, and men, women and children found comfort and new stores of courage in that sturdy face with its firm jaw and massive forehead.

It was not only his own countrymen who responded to his leadership. All the oppressed peoples of Europe felt the spell of his inspiration. Always a good European, he understood their sufferings, and from the BBC his messages went out to all of them. They were honest, magnanimous messages, for he never promised what he could not fulfil. The struggle would be long. Patience and faith were essential, but ultimate victory was certain.

I remember vividly one message to France. It ended with these words: 'Goodnight, then sleep to gather strength for the morning. For the the morning will come. Brightly it will shine on the brave and true, kindly on all who suffer for the cause, and gloriously upon the tombs of heroes. Thus shall shine the dawn. *Vive la France.*'

TRIBUTES FROM THE COMMONWEALTH

'One fire burning in him'

by the Rt Hon. Sir Robert Menzies
Prime Minister of Australia

A tribute paid during the broadcast of the State funeral on 30 January 1965

As this historic procession goes through the streets of London to the Tower Pier, I have the honour of speaking to you from the crypt of St Paul's Cathedral. I do this in two capacities. One is that I, Prime Minister of Australia, happen to be, in point of time, the senior Commonwealth Prime Minister, and therefore speak on behalf of a remarkable world organization which owes more than it can ever express to our departed leader, Sir Winston Churchill. He is one of the famous men whom we thank and praise.

My second capacity is more personal and more intimate. I am sure that you, most of you, have thought about Sir Winston Churchill a great deal, and with warmth in your hearts and in your recollections. Some day, some year, there will be old men and women whose pride it will be to say: 'I lived in Churchill's time'. Some will be able to say: 'I saw him, and I heard him – the unforgettable voice and the immortal words'. And some will be able to say: 'I knew him, and talked with him, and was his friend'.

This I can, with a mixture of pride and humility, say for myself. The memory of this moves me deeply now that he is dead, but is gloriously remembered by me as he goes to his burial amid the sorrow, and pride, and thanks, of all of you who stand and feel for yourselves and for so many millions.

Many of you will not need to be reminded, but some, the younger among you, the inheritors of his master-strokes for freedom, may be glad to be told that your country, and mine, and all the free countries of the world, stood at the very gates of destiny in 1940 and 1941 when the Nazi tyranny threatened to engulf us, and when there was no 'second front' except our own. This was the great crucial moment of modern history. What was at stake was not some theory of government but the whole personal freedom of men, and women, and children. And the battle for them was a battle against great odds. That battle had to be won not only in the air and on the sea and in the field, but in the hearts and minds of ordinary people with a deep capacity for heroism. It was then that Winston Churchill was called, by Almighty God, as our faith makes us believe, to stand as our leader and our inspirer.

There were, in 1940, defeatists, who felt that prudence required submission or such terms as might be had. There were others who, while not accepting the inevitability of defeat, thought that victory was impossible. Winston Churchill scorned to fall into either category, and he was right. With courage, and matchless eloquence, and human understanding, he inspired us and led us to victory.

In the whole of recorded modern history, this was, I believe, the one occasion when one man, with one soaring imagination, with one fire burning in him, and with one unrivalled capacity for conveying it to others, won a crucial victory not only for the forces (for there were many heroes in those days) but for the very spirit of human freedom. And so, on this great day, we thank him, and we thank God for him.

There are two other things I want to say to you, on a day which neither you nor I will ever willingly forget. One is that Winston Churchill was not an institution, but a man; a man of wit and chuckling humour, and penetrating understanding, not a man who spoke to us as from the mountain tops, but one who expressed the simple and enduring feelings of ordinary men and women. It was because he was a great Englishman that he was able to speak for the English people. It was because he was a great Commonwealth statesman that he was able to warm hearts and inspire courage right round the seven seas. It was because he was a great human being that, in our darkest days, he lit the lamps of hope at many firesides and released so many from the chains of despair. There has been nobody like him in our lifetimes. We must, and do, thank God for him, and strive to be worthy of his example.

The second thing I will never forget is this. Winston Churchill's wife is with us here in London; a great and gracious lady in her own right. Could I today send her your love, and mine? She has suffered an irreparable personal loss. But she

The coffin leaving St Paul's Cathedral

has proud and enduring memories. Happy memories, I venture to say. We share her sorrow, but I know that she would wish us to share with her those rich remembrances which the thought of the great man evokes.

There have been, in the course of recorded history, some men of power who have cast shadows across the world. Winston Churchill, on the contrary, was a fountain of light and of hope.

As I end my talk to you from the crypt of St Paul's, with its reminders of Nelson and Wellington, those marvellous defenders of long ago, the body of Winston Churchill goes in procession through the streets of London; *his* London, *our* London, this most historic city, this ancient home of freedom, this place through which, in the very devastation and fire of war, *his* voice rang with courage, and defiance, and hope, and rugged confidence.

His body will be carried on the Thames, a river full of history. With one heart we all feel, with one mind we all acknowledge, that it will never have borne a more precious burden, or been enriched by more splendid memories.

The coffin after it had been placed on the Port of London survey launch Havengore *at Tower Pier for its journey to Festival Pier and Waterloo Station*

78

Memories of the Fulton speech

by the Rt Hon. LESTER PEARSON, Prime Minister of Canada

ALL CANADIANS are grief-stricken by the news of Sir Winston's death. It is hard to believe that this supreme incarnation of the human spirit is now silenced and stilled. Our sympathy and our prayers go out to Lady Churchill, who has shared and strengthened his unparalleled career and whose contribution to that career only Sir Winston himself could fully value.

Despite the inevitability of this day, despite the fullness and sweep of his ninety years, no one who lived through the forties, when his voice inspired free men to their greatest victory, will learn without the deepest sorrow that the end of the road has now been reached by the dominant personality of our century. Sir Winston has passed on, but the example of his courage, the majesty of his voice, the inspiration of his leadership and of his life, these will endure for ever. Defiant in defeat, far-sighted in victory, warm-hearted, high-souled, broad-minded, he was the greatest leader of our time. But he was more than that: his life touched every vital human activity, and mastered most of them. And even though a demi-god, aloof on Olympus, yet the warmest of human beings, with whom it was easy, indeed it was tempting, to identify oneself. That is why his death brings a sense of personal grief and personal loss to millions who never knew or even never saw him. We shall not see his like again. May God rest his great heart and soul.

After paying this tribute the Canadian Prime Minister was interviewed by Leonard Parkin.

LEONARD PARKIN: Everyone who has ever known him seems to have a Winston Churchill story. I am sure you are no exception.

LESTER PEARSON: Yes, every time you met Sir Winston he created a story; and I met him a few times, so I have some stories about him. The one I think of now is when I was ambassador in Washington, Canadian ambassador, and he was coming over after the war to give his Fulton speech, that famous Fulton, Missouri speech, and he thought it might be a good idea if Mr Mackenzie King, who was Prime Minister in Ottawa then, went over and told him what he thought about it – whether he had made any observation that perhaps should have been altered or omitted. And he asked Mr King if he would go over the text of the speech. Mr

King did not want to do that, but he told Mr Churchill, as he then was, that he had an ambassador, a young man in Washington, who knew a lot about the Americans and knew all about Canadian-American things, and he would let the ambassador check the speech. I do not think Mr Churchill thought very much about this, but I was summoned to the British Embassy one Sunday morning to see Mr Churchill by Lord Halifax, who was the ambassador there, and I was ushered into Churchill's bedroom.

He was lying in bed with, as far as I could gather, nothing on. Nothing above the waist at least, which was the only part I saw. He had a big cigar in his mouth and a Scotch on a table at one side – a bed-table that they sometimes used for breakfast – and on the table he had the manuscript of his speech. He gave me a kind of a growling look. He said: 'Your Prime Minister, young man, says you're an authority on American affairs and he thinks you ought to read my speech.' This was rather a frightening introduction for me, and I said: 'Well, I don't know, Sir, but if I can be of any help I'd be glad to.' And he said: 'Well, let's go over it.' I didn't want to do that, because if I went over it with him I would be afraid to make any observation at all. I said: 'Will you let me take it away for an hour and I'll come back? If I have any views, I'll be glad to give them to you.' And he growled: 'Oh, take it away', and went on with his Scotch and his cigar.

I read the speech. It became famous, a historic speech. I thought the introduction was wrong because he referred to the Civil War, and apparently he had assumed that Missouri was in on the northern side in the Civil War. I marked a few changes there. And then he had in his peroration a sentence or paragraph: 'Historians will wonder what to call this war' – or words to that effect – 'I call it the unnecessary war.' I went back with the text and I said: 'Well, Mr Churchill, I don't think much of your introduction; I don't think much of your peroration.' He got quite angry, and I explained to him, and he changed the first paragraph. I said: 'You mustn't call this the unnecessary war because that is what a lot of people in the United States have been saying for some years.' 'Ah', he said, 'I see your point.' He pencilled a few changes, and that was my contribution to the Fulton speech.

PARKIN: Looking back on Churchill's career, how significant a man do you think he was for the strength and development of the Commonwealth?

PEARSON: I should think his greatest contribution will be in other areas than the Commonwealth area. I hope I am not being unfair, but I think he thought of the Commonwealth in terms of the old Commonwealth developing out of the old Empire. I think he was somewhat uncomfortable in the new Commonwealth because of Asian and African membership. He would accept it because he was a realist, and he did accept it of course, but I do not think he would have chosen that future for the Commonwealth. Therefore I think his importance in history is not so much in terms of the Commonwealth as in terms of the world and freedom.

I remember in Ottawa at a dinner where all the Commonwealth High Commissioners were present, after dinner, when he had a brandy, he got very interested

80

in the talk about war – the second war, the first war, and then he got back to the Boer war. And he told some stories about the Boer war which I – and others perhaps – thought were a little unhappy in terms of the fact that the South African High Commissioner was there at that time. He spotted this, after his story, and went up and explained to him how wonderful the Boers had been. He also said something about the colour problem, and then he realized that perhaps in the presence of the Indian High Commissioner, who was sitting beside him, he had not expressed that perfectly. He was anxious to be friendly with all the Commonwealth representatives, and he went up to the Indian High Commissioner afterwards, and I heard him say: 'When you write your Prime Minister, Mr Nehru, tell him I think he is one of the greatest men in contemporary history. He accomplished the two greatest things that a man can accomplish. He has conquered prejudice and he has conquered fear.' The Indian High Commissioner was delighted, and any feeling he may have had that Sir Winston did not appreciate the Asian and African contributions to the Commonwealth were very quickly removed.

PARKIN: Do you think of him as a war-time captain, a soldier-politician, or as a general statesman?

PEARSON: I think of him as a war-time leader, and a war-time statesman, because if it had not been for the opportunity and responsibility he was given in war his position in history would be very different. But I also think of him as a great parliamentarian, a man who, to a greater extent perhaps than any other man, was able to reconcile parliamentary liberty with the necessity of strong government. In time of war, I wonder whether his two greatest achievements were not as a parliamentarian and a war leader, and I would not be too backward in putting the parliamentarian side first.

PARKIN: He seemed to be a happy man. Did you find him this?

PEARSON: Oh, happy – indeed, indeed.

'A Wonderful Man'

by the Rt Hon. K. J. HOLYOAKE,
Prime Minister of New Zealand

THIS IS a sad moment, yet an immensely proud moment, as we pause to pay homage to the memory of a wonderful man. Sir Winston Churchill was an illustrious and greatly loved Englishman, one of the truly great world figures of our day and age. His name will be recorded in history as a man of imperishable words and deeds.

I know that all New Zealand will be moved by feelings of deep regret and sadness at Sir Winston's passing. I have sent a cable to Lady Churchill and her family, expressing our profound sorrow and deepest sympathy to them in this hour of great loss.

At this time, we in New Zealand join with the peoples of Britain and the Commonwealth, and, indeed, the world, in paying affectionate tribute to Sir Winston's memory. This is a moment not so much for mourning as for deep pride and gratitude that, in our time, such a man should have risen among us; that in our hour of gravest peril we could look to such a leader. Here was a man who shaped destiny. Churchill the indomitable, the unconquerable warrior. Churchill, the spirit of a nation, the symbol of freedom and hope for millions of enslaved peoples in the darkest war years. This, surely, is how history will remember him: Churchill in his finest hour as Britain's defiant, implacable, inspiring leader.

During those grim years, it was Churchill who lit the path and guided his country and the free world from the brink of disaster to magnificent victory. Who can measure how great a part of that victory belonged to Churchill's courage and resolution, his dynamic leadership, his momentous, heroic words of encouragement and exhortation? Yet we remember that this was only one facet of the character and achievements of this remarkable man. His talents and vitality were so unbounded that, even outside his singular career as a politician and statesman, he towered above his fellow men: as the dashing young soldier, adventurer, writer; as the eminent author and historian who, in 1953, was awarded the highest recognition in the field of letters, the Nobel Prize for Literature; in his later years, as a painter of exceptional merit. There were no bounds to his interests or his immense capacity. However, it is as one of Britain's greatest parliamentarians that Sir Winston is best loved and remembered.

When he was elected to Parliament in 1900, he was already marked as a young man of brilliant promise. Yet, before that promise found fulfilment, he was to experience in more than full measure the setbacks and disappointments that are the hazards of public life. He was to hold many high offices of state, and he was to know barren years of political adversity. All this went into tempering the character of a man that the nation turned to in its time of need. We cherish the memory of Churchill the incomparable orator, the brilliant debater, and public speaker of wit and puckish good humour; the man of warm virtues and human weaknesses: this is the man who so endeared himself to his people. In his long and incredibly eventful life, Sir Winston Churchill served his country, and his people, with unparalleled distinction, and added a glorious page to the history of our race. This is the man whose imperishable memory we proudly honour today.

Churchill holding open the door of the Queen's car as Her Majesty left Downing Street after attending a dinner party given by Sir Winston and Lady Churchill (seen in doorway) on the occasion of his retirement as Prime Minister, 5 April 1955

Tributes from India

by IVOR JONES, BBC Correspondent in Delhi

INDIA'S PRESIDENT, Sir Sarvepalli Radhakrishnan, O.M., in a message to Queen Elizabeth, spoke of Sir Winston as 'the greatest Englishman we have known'. He said: 'The magic of his personality and his mastery of words renewed faith in freedom in the most difficult years of the Second World War. He left his imprint on the face of Europe and the world. His unforgettable services will be cherished for centuries. I convey to Your Majesty, the British Government and the people of Britain our deepest sympathy in your great loss. It must be some comfort to you to know your grief is shared by millions all over the world'.

Mr Lal Bahadur Shastri, India's Prime Minister, also offered his condolences to Lady Churchill and the British nation. Describing Sir Winston as a man of great initiative and decision, he said: 'He stood for peace and democracy and, in fact, he lived for these objectives until the end'.

There was a time when many Indians saw Sir Winston as the main enemy of their struggle for independence; that was twenty years ago and more. The way this view has changed has been expressed by Mr Krishna Menon, former Defence Minister and Indian High Commissioner in London, and often a bitter critic of Britain. He has described Sir Winston as 'a great fighter, inexorable in his opposition, but a generous opponent'; and as 'a man who never stopped growing, who battled against illness, crises and failures and, at the same time, did not allow victories and triumphs to ride him'. Mr Menon went on: 'Often we have not agreed with him, but he outlived all that and saw the day when he welcomed Pandit Nehru in his own home after the first Commonwealth Prime Ministers' Conference, at which India helped to evolve the formula for Republics in the Commonwealth'.

'Leader in the struggle against Fascism'

by AGHA HILALY, High Commissioner for Pakistan in London

Broadcast in the BBC's Urdu Service on 26 January 1965

SIR WINSTON CHURCHILL was a great man by any standard. Measured whether as a historian, a statesman, a politician, a journalist, an orator or a parliamentarian, Sir Winston qualifies fully for the greatness he has attained not only posthumously as was his right but more fortunately while still alive. Indeed he has become a legend in his own lifetime as his name has been a household word everywhere for more than half a century. He controlled the lives and destinies of millions of peoples both in peace and in war. To his own people he was always a source of strength and pride throughout his long political career, not only when he was at his best as a political orator but even in his later years as a silent member of the House of Commons. A man of deep conviction and indomitable courage he, with his sense of history, fought for what he considered to be right even if this meant he fought alone. He never gave up the struggle nor accepted defeat.

The world will remember Sir Winston not only because he was one of the greatest Prime Ministers and a versatile genius but because of his dynamic leadership in the struggle against Fascism in some of the darkest years of human history. Without him this world would have been a different place to live in. All of us indeed owed to this great man a lasting gratitude for saving humanity from one of the most devastating forms of racial slavery and tyranny that nearly overtook it.

'What Sir Winston Churchill means to me as an African'

by Cosmo Mlongoti

WHAT DOES the name 'Churchill' mean to Africa? My immediate answer to this is just another question – what would Africa be, not to mention Britain, had there not been Churchill? I'm an African from Zambia. I was just about ten in 1944, when I first heard the name of Churchill. I was old enough to know that the world was at war, and that Britain in particular was involved in it. Zambia, then Northern Rhodesia, was a British colony, and as such we were partially involved, and we were equally anxious to see that our side achieved victory. Many young and brave men in my country were recruited as soldiers and went to fight against the Germans, who had already started attacking East African territories, and built a base in the territory now known as Tanzania. Because world peace and stability were at stake, Britain took overwhelming responsibility in informing its alliances of the progress of the war, and it was then that the name of Winston Churchill became a household word even in homes five thousand miles away. It was then that I heard the name of Churchill as a great British war commander. I do remember, quite distinctly, how often people talked about him, how often they read about him and, above all, how often he appeared in British films, which were mainly about the current war. Yes, it was Churchill in almost everything. We were so much afraid of the Germans, and at one time nearly lost hope, when it was said that Churchill intended to have tea in Berlin, meaning, of course, that his troops would take Germany. Such words were a great comfort in many hearts.

Broadcast in 'Calling Central Africa'

Soon the war was over, but the name of Churchill had remained prominent – particularly as it was his victory, the name of Churchill also meant peace. This may sound rather ridiculous, but I very well remember how boys of my age used to play his character, as you find them doing today with cowboy heroes. This was because they knew him, they adored him, and admired his daring character.

In Africa today, particularly in former British colonies, things perhaps would not have been what they are, politically or otherwise, had it not been for Winston Spencer Churchill, his entire devotion to fighting against human suppression, and his desire to bring and preserve human freedom. He died in the early hours of Sunday, 24 January 1965, the man about whom I've heard so much good in history. It's hard to believe, but it's true – all great ones come and go, and Churchill has gone. Grave faces of British people walk solemnly in the streets, wondering whether it's the end of everything or not. But they are not the only ones whose hearts are broken, because I come from Zambia, and I'm just as heartbroken to lose such an outstanding hero of my time, to whom so much is owed by so many.

Visiting the coastal defences in 1940

'My friend, farewell'

by GENERAL DWIGHT D. EISENHOWER, former President of
the United States of America

UPON THE mighty Thames, a great avenue of history, move at this moment to
their final resting place the mortal remains of Sir Winston Churchill. He was a
great maker of history, but his work done, the record closed, we can almost hear
him, with the poet, say:

> Sunset and evening star,
>   And one clear call for me! . . .
> Twilight and evening bell,
>   And after that the dark!
> And may there be no sadness of farewell,
>   When I embark.

This tribute was
broadcast by the
BBC whilst the
coffin was being
carried along the
river during the
last stages of the
State funeral on
30 January 1965

As I, like all other free men, pause to pay a personal tribute to the giant who
now passes from among us, I have no charter to speak for my countrymen –
only for myself. But if, in memory, we journey back two decades to the time when
America and Britain stood shoulder to shoulder in global conflict against tyranny,
then I can presume – with propriety I think – to act as spokesman for the millions
of Americans who served with me and their British comrades during three years
of war in this sector of the earth.

To those men Winston Churchill *was* Britain – he was the embodiment of
British defiance to threat, her courage in adversity, her calmness in danger, her
moderation in success. Among the allies his name was spoken with respect,
admiration, and affection. Although they loved to chuckle at his foibles, they
knew he was a staunch friend. They felt his inspirational leadership. They counted
him a fighter in their ranks. The loyalty that the fighting forces of many nations
here serving gave to him during that war was no less strong, nor less freely given,
than he had, in such full measure, from his own countrymen.

An American, I was one of those allies. During those dramatic months I was
privileged to meet, to talk, to plan, and to work with him for common goals.
Out of that association an abiding – and to me precious – friendship was forged;
it withstood the trials and frictions inescapable among men of strong convictions,
living in the atmosphere of war.

The war ended, our friendship flowered in the later and more subtle tests

88

Churchill with Bernard Baruch (centre) and President Eisenhower at Baruch's home in New York in 1953

imposed by international politics. Then, each of us, holding high official post in his own nation, strove together so to concert the strength of our two peoples that liberty might be preserved among men and the security of the Free World wholly sustained.

Through a career during which personal victories alternated with defeats, glittering praise with bitter criticism, intense public activity with periods of semi-retirement, Winston Churchill lived out his four-score and ten years. With no thought of the length of the time he might be permitted on earth, he was concerned only with the quality of the service he could render to his nation and to humanity. Though he had no fear of death, he coveted always the opportunity to continue that service.

At this moment, as our hearts stand at attention, we say our affectionate, though sad, goodbye to the leader to whom the entire body of free men owes so much.

In the coming years, many in countless words will strive to interpret the motives, describe the accomplishments, and extol the virtues of Winston Churchill – soldier, statesman, and citizen that two great countries were proud to claim as their own. Among all the things so written or spoken, there will ring out through all the centuries one incontestable refrain: here was a champion of freedom.

May God grant that we – and the generations who will remember him – heed the lessons he taught us; in his deeds; in his words; in his life. May we carry on his work until no nation lies in captivity; no man is denied opportunity for fulfilment.

And now, Sir Winston – my friend – farewell!

A visit to Stalin

The Hon. AVERELL HARRIMAN interviewed by LEONARD PARKIN

LEONARD PARKIN: Governor Harriman, you got to know Winston Churchill just about as well as any American did in those early days of the war. What were you doing in Britain at that time, what were your instructions?

AVERELL HARRIMAN: President Roosevelt sent me to London in the early part of 1941 – that was the year that Britain stood alone, and it was the winter you remember when the bombing occurred. President Roosevelt asked me, in rather brief instructions, to make contact with the Prime Minister and the members of the British Government, and report to him what he might do, in order to help Britain keep going.

PARKIN: You would find the then Prime Minister, Churchill, pretty vigorous in his requests, I would think?

HARRIMAN: Yes, very vigorous; and of course he welcomed me as a friend – that was the expression he used the first time I landed. I was taken straight to Chequers, which is where he spent his weekends, and for the next few months I think I spent almost every weekend with him, and he would go over the things he needed. At that time the Battle of the Atlantic was on; he was interested in shipping, and I had an office in the Admiralty. That is when we escorted the convoys half-way across the Atlantic. Then, you remember, food was a bit short, and we tried to get a better diet to the British people. He was interested in every phase of the war – not only the military supplies, for military action, but also what could be done to help the morale of the people. He had a deep affection for the British people and a great appreciation of what they were going through.

PARKIN: Did you see any of the interplay between Churchill and Stalin?

HARRIMAN: Yes, I went with him in August 1942, which was his first visit to Moscow. I was representing the President. Stalin very strongly tried to induce us to start the second front. First he argued with the Prime Minister about why he should do it, and then he got quite insulting. He said if the British were not so cowardly they would start fighting, they would realize that the Nazis were not invincible men. That annoyed the Prime Minister, you can well imagine, and he started in and I think made perhaps one of the most brilliant speeches of his career, because he was stirred up and it was a subject that he knew so well and felt about so deeply. He never quite understood the difficulties of interpretation:

90

he would get carried away. He must have talked for about ten minutes, and then he realized that what he had said had to be interpreted. The poor member of the Embassy staff started to interpret, and the Prime Minister kept nudging him and saying 'Did you tell him this?' and 'Did you tell him that?' It got so confusing that Stalin started to laugh, and said: 'Your words are not important, what is vital is your spirit'. I think that incident gave both men a feeling that they could fight together against the common enemy. Of course both men realized that it was only a war-time relationship and that the Prime Minister's objectives and Stalin's objectives with regard to social and political development were very different.

PARKIN: From where do you think Churchill really drew his great strength, which made him such an incredible leader during the war?

HARRIMAN: His indomitable spirit, his invincible determination to win, and his confidence in Britain, and because he felt by giving inspiration to the British and also to the Americans that we could all work together with a common cause.

PARKIN: Why is he so revered in the United States?

HARRIMAN: I think they recognize his spirit, and of course they have a tremendous affection for him. His humour in talking to the Senate about 'if my mother had been British, my father American, I might have come here under my own right' – remarks of that kind were those that were cherished very much. His Iron Curtain speech at Fulton was very much recognized. But I think he depicts what we all feel is the common heritage of our two countries: the great desire for freedom and independence. They respected him because of his indomitable spirit.

Brother in battle

by PAUL REYNAUD, former Prime Minister of France

CHURCHILL is dead. The whole world is mourning. He was the greatest man of our time. To us Frenchmen he was the one man who after the Armistice in 1940 stood alone against the storm: he saved your country and my country. He was my brother in battle before the war, during the war, after the war.

Before the war we fought together to open the eyes of our governments to the Nazi peril. During the war when I was his mate in misery, as Churchill said, even at the most catastrophic moment never a word of bitterness passed between us. At Dunkirk very few French soldiers had been evacuated. I said to Churchill: 'This is turning to a political question', and, knowing him, I said: 'Do you want me to concentrate the evacuation only on British soldiers?' There were tears in his eyes. He said 'no'; and more than 100,000 French soldiers were evacuated. When the German armoured divisions were slicing France, when the processions of refugees were too much for feeble hearts and rallied the majority against me and my own government, Churchill thought, and I thought too, that his generous offer of a Franco-British union would give me the power to overcome the opposition in my government. Alas, I was the only one in the Cabinet to support the proposal, and the President of the Republic refused to allow me to form a government with those who were determined to fight on.

After the war we served together the European ideal as members of the Consultative Assembly in Strasbourg. I remember one day we were both speaking from a balcony in the Place Kléber in Strasbourg, and Churchill said: 'Are you ready for anything? I'm going to speak French'. He was a great orator. Never to my dying day shall I forget the words of Churchill in his broadcast to France: 'We shall never surrender. We shall continue this struggle until the honour and dignity of France have been restored'. That is a sentence that no Frenchman should ever forget.

'The Passing of a Great Man'

Peter Raleigh, BBC Paris Correspondent
on General de Gaulle's message

On 24 January the flag over the Elysée Palace, official home of General de Gaulle, was at half-mast. At the British Embassy in the Faubourg St Honoré hundreds of French men and women were waiting patiently to sign the book placed there so that they may show their sympathy for the man who, in General de Gaulle's words, 'was the greatest in the greatest drama of the last war'.

Those words occurred in the French President's message of sympathy to the Queen. To Lady Churchill, General de Gaulle wrote, 'From the bottom of our hearts, my wife and I share the deep affliction which has come to you and yours, to England, and to men of feeling throughout the world. In France Sir Winston's death has been deeply felt everywhere. As for me, in the passing of this great man, I lose a companion in war and a friend'.

Those who know General de Gaulle will know how sincerely felt his tribute was. In his war memoirs he recounts how, in spite of all the war-time clashes he had with Sir Winston, Sir Winston had seemed to him from beginning to end the great champion of a great enterprise, a great artist of a great history.

It was in November 1958 that General de Gaulle gave Sir Winston the one thousand and fifty-fourth Cross of the Liberation saying, 'I want Sir Winston to know this – today's ceremony simply means that France knows what she owes him'.

A Loss for the Free World

by Dr Konrad Adenauer, formerly Chancellor of the
German Federal Republic

THE DEATH of Sir Winston Churchill is not only a great and terrible loss for the British people but is also a loss for the whole of the free world and especially for the German people. In the course of his political activity since the war Churchill repeatedly emphasized how essential it was to create European unity. He had spoken of it for the first time at Zürich in 1946. I first met him when I was a member of a German delegation at a European conference at The Hague in 1948. Churchill then greeted us Germans in a friendly, kindly and forthcoming way. And again in the following years, when I met him repeatedly, he always showed the same friendliness both towards the German people and to me personally. I spoke to him last in the early part of 1955 on the Riviera when we had a long, entirely friendly and intimate discussion which covered the latest problems of the world at the time. The history of our times is unimaginable without his work and personality. With deep respect we offer our condolences and sympathy at this moment to Lady Churchill and the family of the deceased. I do this on behalf of the German people. I venture to do so also on my own behalf, for during the whole time that I knew Sir Winston Churchill he always received me with nothing but friendliness and kindness.

Broadcast in the German Service of the BBC

Dr Adenauer, Federal German Chancellor, shaking hands with Sir Winston after lunching with him at Downing Street (May 1953)

Working with Churchill

by LORD BRIDGES, Secretary to the Cabinet throughout the
War of 1939–1945

WHEN Winston Churchill became Prime Minister in May 1940, to my surprise
I found myself brought into the small group of those who worked closely with
him – staff officers and civil servants, advisers and secretaries. I want to speak of
the relationship which he established with those who worked for him, for in this, as
in so many ways, he was not like any other man. In his dealings with those helpers
whom he gathered round him, a special quality or attitude of mind showed itself.
It was something so distinctive that there is no single word to describe it. Generosity
was a large part of it. Friendliness too; and he could be devastatingly outspoken
about the work in hand to a degree which implied immense confidence in us.

But perhaps I can explain it better against the background of how he worked.
There were no frontiers between home and office, between work hours and the
rest of the day; work went on everywhere, in his study, in the dining-room, in his
bedroom. A summons would come at almost any hour of the day or night to
help in some job. Minutes would be dictated, corrected, re-dictated. One might
find oneself unexpectedly sitting in the family circle or sharing a meal while one
took his orders. Or there were the occasional invitations to Chequers to dine and
sleep on the pretext of some piece of work. In this way, the group of those with
whom he worked most were given, as it were, honorary membership of his
household; we became his familiars.

> 'The friends thou hast, and their adoption tried,
> Grapple them to thy soul with hoops of steel.'

Oh yes. We were grappled with hoops of steel, but we all submitted very
willingly. And I'm sure he did it, not like Polonius from cool calculation, but
because it was his instinct to work in this way. He liked to have round him a
small group, some with brains to tap, others to be sent scurrying round to verify
facts and figures. He knew, too, that he could work best if those in the circle were
congenial to him and felt at their ease.

This same quality, which as a kind of shorthand I will call his generosity of
mind, showed itself in the free way in which he exposed the rough workings of his
thoughts. As soon as an idea struck him, he would dictate a draft, he would have
six copies made and would shoot them out for comments. And what did one do if
suddenly asked to comment on a draft on some question of high policy? How far

could one go? Yes, it could be rather daunting. But the answer, as so often with him, was quite simple when once you had found it. So long as you were in sympathy with him, so long as you were trying to help, he would listen in a very kindly way to your suggestions however foolish and feeble they might be. But if he felt that the tide or current of your thoughts was flowing directly against his tide, he would easily become impatient of one's comments.

All this was tremendous fun and made the days full of excitement. Moreover, it was of the greatest value, for it showed us so clearly how his mind worked and what he was aiming at. And perhaps this, too, explains the way in which he imposed himself on one, if that is the right way to put it. He might send me to see someone on his behalf and to arrange for some business to be carried out in a certain way. On such an occasion I always felt that he trusted me completely to carry out the instructions he had given me down to the smallest detail. Having given me the order, he had dismissed the matter from his mind as though he had completed the task himself. One felt oneself for the moment to be an extra and detachable limb of his. And so, when sometimes it turned out to be impossible to do what he had said, I always felt most uncomfortable until I had told him that his orders had not been exactly carried out and the reasons why. So close was the bond of sympathy and allegiance that he established, indeed, that he sometimes expected you to know what he wanted done before he had told you. And even that was not nearly as extravagant as it may sound.

Leaving Buckingham Palace for the Coronation of Queen Elizabeth II. He is wearing the uniform of Lord Warden of the Cinque Ports

96

You may say that this is only a description of how a man of genius got the best out of his staff. No doubt that was part of it, but that is certainly not the impression that I want to leave. When I look back on the work done by those in close association with him, through the unbroken strain of five long war years, it seems fantastic to suppose that we should have done what we did, and have thrived on it and enjoyed it and have known while we toiled away that this was the time of our lives, that we should never again enjoy any work so much. In retrospect, I see more clearly how all this was achieved. I know now that, besides compelling in us the utmost devotion, besides inspiring us all and creating through his strong sympathy a degree of comradeship the like of which I have never known before, besides all this, he communicated to us something of his own matchless determination and courage, something of his own vitality and stamina.

An idealistic picture. Was it always like this? No, of course it was not. There were moments when he did things which maddened us, though never, let me add, in the great crises of the war. And at times he gave decisions which seemed to us stupid, although years later I have sometimes seen in a flash why he did certain things which at the time were incomprehensible to me. There were times too when the sun went down, when the bond of sympathy had snapped, and one was left in darkness, out in the cold for days, perhaps for a week or more. But so far as I was concerned, it always ended in the same way. I would be sent for one morning and as I went into his room I would see at once that the sun was high in the heavens again. And while he told me what he wanted me to do, he would, almost gruffly, even shyly, slip in two or three words in quite a different tone of voice – only a few words – but they would have such a warmth of feeling and affection that one knew that, come what might, nothing else in the world mattered except that one should go on working for him.

Imaginative man of action

by SIR FITZROY MACLEAN, M.P.

Broadcast in the European Services of the BBC

I HEARD of Winston Churchill's death from a shepherd at home. 'The old gentleman's away,' he said; and then added: 'He was in every way a man of parts.'

His words, so apt in their simplicity, brought back a whole range of varied memories. Winston at Chartwell in the summer just before the war, indignant and fractious at the follies and blunders of the government, grumpily throwing ants' eggs to the goldfish. Winston in the First Lord's flat at the Admiralty a few months later, already transfigured by the need and the opportunity for action. Then a succession of other war-time encounters. In Egypt with his generals before Alamein, even then finding time to help us plan raids behind Rommel's lines in the Western Desert. At Chequers in the summer of 1943, when he briefed me for my mission to Yugoslavia. In Cairo the same winter. At Marrakesh during his convalescence. On the radio-telephone from London to Algiers via Washington in an unnerving conversation when neither of us was clear whether we were talking in code or not. Back in England just before D-Day. In Naples with Tito on the terrace of Queen Victoria's villa or swimming far out in the waters of the Bay. Then after the war, at Chartwell and Chequers and No. 10. And, finally, last summer, in the smoking room of the House of Commons, when we had a drink together and I felt it might be the last time I saw him.

The circumstances of these meetings varied. Sometimes they were official. Sometimes only his family were there. Sometimes his surroundings were military and sometimes parliamentary. Sometimes he was wearing one of his uniforms; or loose white ducks; or bathing pants; or a black coat and striped trousers; or sitting up in bed and smoking a cigar; or wearing a zipped-up boiler suit and slippers. But always, whatever his surroundings and whatever his state of dress or undress, he was an immensely impressive, indeed an awe-inspiring figure. And always he was at pains to see that his visitor was comfortable and copiously provided with food and drink and anything else he might require – in one instance, when I had been kept unexpectedly late, a suit of his own silk underclothes to sleep in.

As often as not, the domestic and the official would merge one into the other, and generals and cabinet ministers who had been summoned to a planning session would find themselves sitting through a comic film before they got down

98

With Marshal Tito of Yugoslavia when they met in Naples, 1944

to the night's work. And once the immediate task was completed – sometimes even before – their host would turn to lighter topics, reciting poetry, telling stories, or even bursting into song. 'What,' I once asked Marshal Tito, 'struck you most about Mr Churchill?' 'His humanity,' he answered. 'Not like Stalin?' I said. 'Not like Stalin,' came the reply.

'In every way,' said the shepherd on that far Scottish hillside, 'a man of parts.' Civilization's ideal in the Renaissance was the complete man. It is an ideal which in this age of technocrats and specialists seems very remote, but which was never more fully attained than by Winston Churchill. He was a man of deeds, but also a thinker and a man of words. A planner and a man of fruitful imagination, who carried his plans into action. He was not only a statesman: he was a soldier, a writer, a painter, a farmer, a racehorse owner, a bricklayer, and a polo player. And, whatever he did, he did with the same immense spirit, gusto, conviction, and enjoyment, with the resolute determination of the true fighter, the true man of action. He loved life. He was a man of intense feeling. Firm as a rock himself, he never lacked compassion for others. And last but not least, he was a romantic.

Through all the stresses and strains of his career he was constantly helped and cheered and sustained by his devoted wife, who brought to the task all her immense love and tact together with a strength and courage that equalled his own. She and his family played an immensely important part in his life, and my recent memories are of him surrounded by his grandchildren, who caused him intense pride and pleasure.

It was his love of life and action, coupled with his unceasing interest in almost every form of human activity, that made him want to join in everything himself, especially if any danger or excitement were involved. After his resignation from the government in 1915 he went straight from the Cabinet to serve as a regimental officer in the front line in France. In 1944, at seventy, only a direct order from his

99

Sovereign prevented him from landing in France on D-Day. And to Tito in German-occupied Yugoslavia, he wrote in a message of which I was the bearer: 'I wish I could come myself, but I am too old and heavy to jump out on a parachute'. And I am sure that he meant it.

Guerrilla warfare and irregular operations of all kinds had a natural fascination for him. They had a romantic and picturesque side which appealed to him. They recalled, too, his own early experiences and adventures in Cuba and South Africa, at Omdurman and on the North-west frontier of India. And he devoted to them what his senior advisers sometimes considered a disproportionate amount of time and attention. For those of us, however, who were fighting this particular war it was deeply reassuring to know of his interest in our affairs.

With his indomitable courage and passionate love of freedom, perhaps Winston Churchill's greatest gift was his sense of history. This led him to look not only to the past, but, with a foresight denied to lesser men, steadily and penetratingly into the future. It enabled him to see people and policies in their true proportion. It enabled him to combine so outstandingly the qualities of the thinker and the man of action, of the statesman and the soldier, and it endowed him with the vision without which true greatness is impossible.

Now that he has gone and that we face an uncertain future without him, we cannot do better than bear constantly in mind the words of his victory broadcast, in which he warned us 'not to fall back into the rut of inertia and confusion and the craven fear of being great'. It is a danger that certainly threatens us today.

The three-power Yalta Conference (February 1945): Churchill with Roosevelt and Stalin in the grounds of Livadia Palace

A dominant personality

by Lt Gen. SIR IAN JACOB, K.B.E., C.B., Military Assistant Secretary to the War Cabinet 1939–1946

Broadcast in the European Services of the BBC

Another tribute by Sir Ian Jacob is on page 56 above

WHEN I think of Sir Winston Churchill I find it difficult to focus my mind and to concentrate my thoughts. To give a concise impression of such a man is as difficult as to take a photograph with a small camera of a whole range of mountains: one is defeated by the size and complexity of the subject.

I remember him first as a Minister in Chamberlain's War Cabinet, called back on the outbreak of war to run the Admiralty. I did not see in him then the power that he developed when he was given the leadership. Courage, industry, drive – yes, but with these qualities seemed to go a perverseness that made life difficult for his colleagues. But once he had been entrusted with the supreme post all these awkward characteristics became suddenly irrelevant – without the slightest difficulty he became dominant, and he seemed to move forward with complete certainty.

He was confronted at first with nothing but disaster. France was being overrun, all Europe seemed lost to Hitler's irresistible armies. And Dunkirk seemed likely to be the cemetery of the British Army. While not minimizing the crisis nor indulging in foolish optimism, Churchill remained as firm as a rock. His speeches conveyed determination to the world, but they were not mere words covering an inner weakness. In the small circle which bore the responsibility with him he was cool, tireless, pugnacious and imaginative. He seemed to be borne up by his sense of history, and by his vast experience of great events. With him at our head, nothing seemed impossible.

His method of work has often been described; it depended upon the sleep which he took for about five hours in the early morning and one hour in the afternoon. With this régime, and with his complete concentration on the task in hand, he could day after day and week after week do as much in one day as most men could do in three. Nothing was too much trouble; nothing that was important was postponed; no detail which he thought was worth pursuing was beneath his notice. Thus every aspect of the war effort was stimulated and his personality penetrated the whole national framework. After a year of office, and after much trial and tribulation, he was established as the personification of Britain, supreme in the hearts and minds of all his countrymen.

Then came the test of alliance. First Russia and then the United States were dragged into the war, which became world-wide. Churchill found himself one of the three men who between them controlled the destinies of the Allies. I was one of the very few who were present at his early meetings with Roosevelt in the White House and with Stalin in the Kremlin. Both these men controlled forces which gradually overshadowed our own in strength, and they were conscious of their power. Churchill by sheer personality held his own in that company and, with his grasp of military affairs and his deep knowledge of Europe, he often seemed pre-eminent. He guided Roosevelt, while giving him due deference as a Head of State, and he understood, as Roosevelt did not, the true nature of Stalin and of the Communist objectives. If Churchill had had his way, and had been supported by the full weight of American power, Europe would now have been in a far healthier state.

Churchill was not an armchair strategist. He was above all a man of action, never happy unless he had a project to drive forward with his incomparable fire. Through five long years he never flagged, leading, encouraging, prodding and inspiring. This was the secret of his success as a leader in war and no doubt the reason why he was thrown from power when the load was removed by victory. He was too fiery to hold his place when ordinary men desired to resume the domestic squabbles of peace-time politics. As time goes on his actions will be analysed and criticized, but nothing will diminish the glory of the man who saved the country he loved so deeply, who upheld the cause of Europe, and who by his example inspired the free world. Nor can anything dim for those who served him the awe and reverence he inspired.

Churchill in Athens, 1944

by ROBERT MATHEW, M.P.

*Broadcast in the
BBC German Service*

IN DECEMBER 1944, British troops were besieged in Athens. I was commanding a unit there and the ELAS were at the gates of the city determined to set up a left-wing dictatorship. It was a terribly cold winter, we were without light or heat and on half rations. The fighting was bitter.

Suddenly Mr Churchill announced he was coming to Athens. He wanted to mediate between ELAS and the legitimate Greek Government. On my suggestion, General Scobie, the British Commander-in-Chief, tried to persuade Mr Churchill to hold his meeting on British soil – in the cruiser H.M.S. *Ajax* which was lying off the Piraeus. We received a sharp reply. 'I shall come ashore at Navy Point as arranged. The enemy are to come over under a flag of truce. After the conference I wish to be taken to a point of vantage where I can view the battle.'

I was made responsible for the Prime Minister's safety while ashore. I raced in my staff car to Navy Point and noted that there were several enemy machine-guns on the road between G.H.Q. and the port.

Winston Churchill eventually landed and climbed slowly, oh! so slowly, up the steep steel ladder that led to the armoured vehicle I had waiting for him. I remember thinking how old and tired he looked as he climbed. But when he got to the top and I saluted him, I looked into his face; and realized here was a man younger and with greater energy than us all – and he was seventy even then.

Before he could climb into his armoured car, a shell landed within twenty-five feet. 'What was that?' he asked me rather fiercely. I explained it was an Italian 75 mm. captured by the ELAS troops. A slow and pleased grin came into his face. 'What! Shelling me – damned cheek!' he said. The smell of grape-shot had swept away all the weariness of long Cabinet meetings and the dusty government offices in London; he was a young officer again. As we drove through the machine-gun fire towards central Athens I told him that my father nearly fifty years before had also been under fire with him at the Battle of Omdurman. That pleased the old lion.

When we reached the British Embassy, I knew there was a fixed line machine-gun covering the entrance. As he slowly walked up the steps somebody shouted, *'Zito! Churchill'* – 'Hurrah for Churchill'. He stopped. He slowly turned and held up his fingers in a Victory salute. I was horrified and told him to go on. 'Why should I?' – 'Because this is a hot spot. Somebody was killed on these steps this morning.' He did nothing, and I pushed him physically up the steps, saying, 'Sir, I am responsible for your safety and I order you indoors!' He gave me a fierce thunderous look which I shall never forget.

The conference with the ELAS leaders took place in a large conference room in the Foreign Affairs Ministry, lighted by very dim hurricane lanterns. It was bitterly cold and we were wrapped in thick coats. Eventually I brought the enemy representatives into the room. The members of the Greek Government scowled but Churchill rose and said very solemnly, 'Gentlemen – we will rise to greet the enemy'. He then addressed the conference. It was a moment of great drama. I remember the feeble light flickering against the heavy mahogany furniture of the room and the strange gathering, which included the present Prime Minister of Greece, Papandreou, and other Greek Ministers, Macmillan, Eden, Field-Marshal Alexander, and battle-stained soldiers from the British, the Greek, and the ELAS armies. Above stood the indomitable figure of the greatest leader of them all – pleading for peace against the background of gunfire. Another piece of history was being added to the great and long story of the old, old city.

Conference with ELAS leaders in Athens in December 1944: Churchill with Archbishop of Athens; behind them are British and Greek representatives including Mr Macmillan and Mr Eden

The end of an era

LORD BOOTHBY, in an interview with NICHOLAS BARRETT

*Broadcast in
'This Time of Day'
(Home Service)
on 26 January 1965*

BARRETT: Lord Boothby, you've said that the death of Sir Winston Churchill marks the end of an era. How does it mark the end of an era?

LORD BOOTHBY: Oh well, he said, you know, that the history of mankind was the history of war. He lived his own life in terms of war, not, I think, by choice, but that's how it went. That's no longer true. If we have another war on a major scale it's not the history of mankind, it's the end of mankind, and that is why I said that it marked the end of an era. I don't think we shall ever live again in terms of battleships and cruisers and destroyers and cavalry charges – he even went back to that. It lasted right through from India, through Africa, and Cuba. He was a fighter all his life, and a fighter not in political terms but a fighter in actual terms. And I think that is absolutely finished.

BARRETT: Surely this finished in 1945 and he stayed on twenty years into another era?

LORD BOOTHBY: Yes, he stayed on, but you've used the right expression – stayed on is exactly what you mean, and what in fact happened. But he wasn't part of it. He had one or two very good ideas after the war. That's why I think it was a mistake he became Prime Minister again. He confused ephemeral political power with permanent historical fame. He could never once again scale the heights that he had done, and I think he should have been a sort of philosopher king, and his ideas would have had much greater force. But these ideas – I'm referring really to the idea of a united Europe under British leadership – which he was the first to launch – and also a very close association between the Anglo-Saxon peoples – could both have been done, and both been achieved. The Fulton speech and the Zürich speech were tremendous in their way, but when he became Prime Minister he hesitated to commit this country to any very definite course because he didn't want to make a mistake. I don't blame him altogether. I understand it. But he didn't do anything, and therefore I regard Churchill's effective career as stopping with victory.

BARRETT: You worked with him for three years as Parliamentary Private Secretary. He was certainly a man of wit; but was he a man with a sense of humour?

LORD BOOTHBY: No. He hadn't got a humorous outlook on life. I don't think he could have done the things he did if he had had a humorous outlook on life. He could never certainly have induced the sublime spirit – as he called it himself – in this country in 1940 if he'd had a sense of humour. I think he had to have something much more than that. Myself I've always believed and said that a humorous outlook on life gave you the best life, and I think I've got it myself. But Churchill hadn't got a humorous outlook on life. He had a marvellous gift of repartee and he was very witty on many occasions, but a deep, underlying sense of humour he never had, because he felt about everything too seriously for that.

BARRETT: Do you regret the passing of this era that ended in 1945?

LORD BOOTHBY: Oh no, I thank God for it. I really do, because I agree with Freud who was a deep pessimist, that the advent of the atomic bomb, when thirty years before it was invented – or twenty-five years at any rate – he said – 'Men have reached a point when they could by using the powers they've got and have invented, exterminate themselves to the last man, and I think that probably', he said, 'confronted by the choice between complete self-annihilation and survival they may opt for survival.' I think that is true. I think to stop this spirit of aggression, this war that Churchill rightly said has been the characteristic of the whole of human history, I think they had to do something which would make war not worth while. I don't think that we can live any longer in terms of war, and as I said at the beginning, Churchill has perforce had to live his whole life in terms of war. We shall emerge, in due course, into the sunlight of a better life for everybody concerned; more enjoyment, more fun, more gaiety, more happiness.

BARRETT: How is this going to happen?

LORD BOOTHBY: I really dismiss the danger of nuclear warfare. I think the greatest danger that confronts mankind at the moment is what they call the population explosion. I think we've really got to bring that under control, and in order to do it we've got to bring first of all the religious superstitions, particularly in India and the Far East, under control, and bring birth under control. But if we can do that, then I see a reasonable life ahead of all of us. I'm more optimistic than I've ever been since I entered public life.

The Vision of a United Europe

by SIR STEPHEN KING-HALL

Broadcast in
'This Time of Day'
(*Home Service*)

WINSTON CHURCHILL was a man of infinite variety and versatility. I have only felt justified in accepting the honour of saying a few words about him because I think I may throw some beams of light on certain aspects of his character which have been obscured by the image of the great war leader.

I cannot claim to have been more than one of thousands who had dealings with him, but we had some contacts during the years when I shared his passionate conviction that the nation must be aroused to the reality of the Nazi menace; I was a colleague of his in the famous war-time Parliament and I was closely associated with him in the United Europe movement.

As I look back on talks I had with him, the parts of his character which remain vividly in my mind are his humanity and his boyishness. I always felt that the rather mischievous schoolboy was waiting in a corner of his complex character ready to jump out and have a bit of fun.

One day in 1944 Sir John Anderson, the Prime Minister and I were talking and Sir John gave Churchill a great lecture bristling with statistics about the need to modernize our road system after the war. The Prime Minister became very bored and turning to me said:

'Captain! Would you agree that I have motored as many miles in the kingdom during the war as any man?'

I replied: 'I should think so.'

'Then,' said Churchill as he waved his cigar in the air, 'let me tell you *both* that I have never *once* been held up on the roads. They seem quite adequate to me.'

Turning to me, the Prime Minister winked as much as to say, 'That will stop this lecture.' It did.

Most people think of Churchill as a great war leader though historians may debate whether David Lloyd George had the harder task.

Of Churchill from his earliest days it can be said with some degree of truth 'war was his business'. But was the organization and participation in destruction his heart's desire? I am sure it was not. His humanity – he was a Liberal of the Whig variety – could only be satisfied by the achievement of a great constructive project.

*Graham Sutherland's
portrait of Sir
Winston Churchill*

Against the record of his triumphs in the balance sheet of his life must be set the tragedy that he never knew the satisfaction of a great non-violent triumph.

Why did Churchill so dislike the famous 'Sutherland' picture of the craggy, tough and almost brutal man of war? I believe it was because it is a picture of the façade behind which was concealed the real, the inner, the almost secret Churchill.

When he suffered the bitter and unexpected defeat in 1945, it may have been because the electorate instinctively felt that he was not the man for the great task of reconstruction.

I believe he said to himself: 'I will show them I can be a great builder' and he launched the crusade for a United Europe under British leadership. Here I can speak with authority because he asked me to join his original small committee of which I was at one period the honorary secretary. Once a week I saw him alone in his room in the House. It is here that I have seen him with tears rolling down his cheeks as he spoke of the bombing of the German cities. I was awe-struck to find myself the recipient of moving confidences about his personal feelings and I realized how passionately he felt about the need to re-build Europe, and I was amazed to find myself answering him that short of being a complete pacifist, the bombing was unavoidable. I realized that I was in the presence of a very different Churchill from that of the popular image.

This was not the Churchill of 'the blood, toil, sweat and tears' or 'we will fight them on the beaches' oratorical performances. This was a humble Churchill deeply distressed by man's inhumanity to man; a Churchill asking himself in my presence some spiritual questions so personal it would be a breach of confidence to particularize them.

He toiled mightily for the cause. He brought Dr Adenauer and the Germans

On the steps of the new House of Europe building in Strasbourg before the second general assembly of the Council of Europe, August 1950: left to right, M. Paul-Henri Spaak, M. Paul Reynaud, Churchill, and M. Schuman (French Foreign Minister)

back to the high table of the democracies at the famous Congress at The Hague of which I was the honorary press officer.* This conference forced the opponents of the United Europe movement in Paris and Whitehall, amongst the French Socialists, the British Labour Government and elements in the Tory party, to swallow the creation of the Council of Europe.

At Strasbourg, at the Council, Churchill made his great speech demanding a European army. Paul Reynaud was with difficulty restrained from moving that Churchill should be elected the first C. in C.

Churchill said to me: 'We must not go too fast but we have started a movement which will sweep through Europe like a prairie fire'.

Nine months later Churchill was once more Prime Minister. Expectations ran high. Now – so we on the executive committee supposed and all our European friends anticipated – there will be a great leap forward. Alas! the Churchill Government did *not* make United Europe the spearhead of its foreign policy. Our leader, it seemed, had abandoned the battle at the very moment we expected a general offensive. I think I can now reveal we had a private message from Churchill urging us to continue the campaign.

What went wrong? There is no time nor is this the moment to do much more than answer the question: 'Did Churchill not really believe in the cause?' The answer is, he believed in it passionately. I can give you a hint and I quote a remark Churchill once made to me in a different context.

He said to me, 'The party machine was too strong for me'. So the great attempt he made to end his career with something peaceful and constructive failed. A personal tragedy for Churchill and, as we were to find out ten years later, perhaps a disaster for the nation. If Churchill's vision of a United Europe created and led by Britain had materialized, many problems which now beset us would never have arisen.

I will end my humble tribute to a side of the character of this remarkable man which perhaps has been overlooked, by quoting what he said to me in 1942. It has relevance today.

'There is much gratitude towards us because we stood alone. It will not last. When we have beaten the Nazis we shall have to take our coats off and work for our livings. Never forget King-Hall we have to import 50 per cent of what we eat.' Then came the schoolboy smile as he added: 'If the *scrunch* came, I very much fear that notwithstanding our admirable constitutional arrangements it would be difficult to decide in a peaceful manner which half of the population should eat and which should starve.'

I wonder, if Churchill was with us today in the plenitude of his powers, whether he would be exerting his influence to promote that national unity in time of crisis of which he was the inspiration and symbol from 1940 to 1945?

* See the tribute by Dr Adenauer page 94 above

Churchill as a Painter

by SIR GERALD KELLY, K.C.V.O., former President of the
Royal Academy (in an interview with HUGH MORAN)

*Broadcast in
'This Time of Day'
(Home Service)*

MORAN: Sir Gerald – what sort of a painter was Sir Winston?

SIR GERALD KELLY: He was jolly good. Hang it all. He painted exactly like I paint. We both did our best. We both enjoyed it. And he wasn't an artist; he was a painter. I'm not an artist, I'm a painter.

MORAN: And what's the difference?

SIR GERALD KELLY: I don't know. I don't understand art. And when they talk to me about art, it's terrifying. But painting is getting the right colour, putting it in the right place, as the great Degas said.

MORAN: Do you think Sir Winston would have been recognized as a painter if he hadn't been called Sir Winston Churchill?

SIR GERALD KELLY: If he had become a painter – a professional – as he became a politician – I should have thought he would certainly have been. He painted a lot of jolly good pictures. And he painted well. Now, when I became President I had a friend who was a great great friend of Sir Winston's called Edward Marsh, who liked pictures and collected them; and I said to Eddie, 'Look here, the pictures Winston sent to the Academy last year were not much good.' And he said, 'Come with me, I'll take you down to Chartwell and you shall have it out with him.' So down we went. Had a jolly good lunch; and he laughed – so gay. Of course, I was frightened and . . . but you couldn't go on being frightened of Winston especially as we both talked about painting.

MORAN: Did you criticize any of his paintings then?

SIR GERALD KELLY: No more than I would criticize anybody else's paintings. No. I looked and then when I liked one I said how very nice it was. And I saw what I think is his best picture. I think it is one of the best pictures painted in England – I'm quite serious. I think it is one of the best pictures painted in England in my lifetime.

MORAN: What's that one, Sir Gerald?

SIR GERALD KELLY: *Snow at Chartwell.* That was painted in 1924. It is an absolute smasher. It's one of the coldest pictures. I don't know that I would have wanted to have painted it, because I would have been so cold. But it's quite marvellous. Marvellous.

MORAN: How long had Sir Winston been painting at that time – 1924?

SIR GERALD KELLY: I think he'd been painting for a very long time. Eddie Marsh told me he'd been painting for forty-five or fifty years.

MORAN: What did he think of himself as a painter?

SIR GERALD KELLY: He liked it, you know. He liked doing it. I want you to understand that Winston was naturally a painter and he painted, and the word 'art' was never mentioned.

MORAN: When he came to the Royal Academy to look at paintings how did he behave? What sort of paintings did he look at?

SIR GERALD KELLY: Oh sweet – he really was absolutely sweet. I used to take him round and we used to stroll round after the dinner, you know, but I never noticed him looking very much at other people's pictures.

MORAN: He looked at his own most of the time?

SIR GERALD KELLY: Well – he looked at his own with great care and he complained if they were not hung exactly as he liked them. And then he strolled on round the rest and I don't think he was very interested. I have seen more famous painters than Sir Winston Churchill behave in exactly the same way.

Bottlescape (c.1932): a painting by Churchill

Churchill as a Historian and Man of Letters

by F. W. DEAKIN, Warden of St Antony's College, Oxford, and formerly one of Sir Winston Churchill's literary assistants

Broadcast in the European Services of the BBC; other appreciations of Churchill as a historian are on pages 48, 52-54 above

SIR WINSTON'S historical imagination was unfettered by exposure to a formal higher education. His broad vision of events was not only fresh and impressionistic, but also severely ordered in a studied pattern.

His first major work in this progress is the biography of his father, Lord Randolph Churchill, the sensitive and warm study of a family and social background. It was written after his own first exciting experience as a Member of the

Chartwell, Churchill's country home at Westerham, Kent

House of Commons, and this enriched his historical interpretation of Lord Randolph's career. In a moving tribute to his father, Sir Winston wrote in 1951:

> I believe he could take his place in the House of Commons today with less sense of disharmony than any of his contemporaries. 'Trust the people'; 'I have never feared the English democracy'; are themes which claim more general acceptance than when he set them forth.

From the hills of India to the Nile Valley, from Khartoum to the campaigns of the Boer War, the march of Sir Winston's writings deploys through Blenheim and Westminster into the history of the conduct of war on all the battle-fronts of 1914–18. His *World Crisis*, published in 1921, is an olympian saga, penetrating in its judgment of decisions and mistakes in high places, and above all – and here, perhaps, lies his genius as a historian in the strict sense of the word – his sensitive, intuitive understanding of how decisions of state are made and the virtues and weaknesses of those who make them.

Sir Winston was no believer in the lessons of history as a substitute for political judgment. The pages of this great book represent the height of his own special art of narrative. As, for example, on the mobilization of the Royal Navy on the eve of the First World War:

> We may now picture this great Fleet, with its flotillas and cruisers, steaming slowly out of Portland Harbour, squadron by squadron, scores of gigantic castles of steel wending their way across the misty, shining sea, like giants bowed in anxious thought. We may picture them again as darkness fell, eighteen miles of warships running at high speed and in absolute blackness through the narrow Straits, bearing with them into the broad waters of the North the safeguard of considerable affairs.

The life of John, first Duke of Marlborough, was published in the years between 1933 and 1938 – between the accession to power of Hitler and the Munich Pact. Written during the lean years of Sir Winston's own political isolation, this massively documented work with its imaginative and passionate interpretation is the supreme example of Sir Winston's capacity as a historian to identify himself with his theme. For him, the essential drama of the story lay in the contrast between the glory and importance of Marlborough's deeds, and (as Sir Winston puts it) 'the small regard of his countrymen for his memory'.

The genesis of this biography lies in Sir Winston's early reading, in frontier days in India, of Lord Macaulay, whose aspersions on the public conduct and loyalties of the Duke had been a smouldering source of irritation to the young Churchill. He was now determined, in his own words, 'to pin the word "Liar" to Macaulay's genteel coat-tails'. It is the general view that he succeeded. This book also reveals Sir Winston's resounding view of the role of the hero in history. It is the fate of great men to be exposed to authors. They must not shirk the process.

Perhaps the most revealing example of Sir Winston's ideas on the vision of British history from the fixed distances of the past to the shifting sands of the present, is his *A History of the English-Speaking Peoples*. Started in 1938 and

The Battle of Blenheim: tapestry in Blenheim Palace

completed after the interruption of the Second World War, it belongs as much to his own biography as to his contribution to history.

I write about the things in our past that appear significant to me, and I do so as one not without some experience of historical and violent events in our own time.

In the debates on the past he is often far from impartial. To him, every episode in the island story has its heroes and its villains. For example, King Richard III never – according to Sir Winston – murdered the Princes in the Tower; he was the victim of a monstrous falsification by Tudor hacks at Court.

I remember on one occasion just before the Second World War an argument conducted with energetic brutality and disarming kindliness as to whether or not King Alfred ever burnt the cakes. Sir Winston explained that at times of crisis myths were often of more historical importance than the evidence: that the cakes symbolized a myth of British resistance in their sternest hour against the Saxon invader, and the source of inspiration to those dim, distant figures, the Counts of the Saxon shore, striving to defend the island. I was duly chastened, and shortly afterwards, with inexorable historical logic, Sir Winston was to find himself the lineal and supreme successor of those Counts of the Saxon shore – at Dunkirk –

and as the leader of the most decisive British resistance in her history. But this time no myth was needed.

On the long journey upon which Sir Winston, as he wrote of John, Duke of Marlborough with beguiling understatement, 'had marched by unexpected paths', the last milestone is marked by the six volumes on the Second World War. This work is the literary expression of his Finest Hour, as he wrote in the first preface:

> I doubt whether any similar record exists or has ever existed of the day-to-day conduct of war and administration. I do not describe it as history, for that belongs to another generation. But I claim with confidence that it is a contribution to history which will be of service to the future.

It was for a brief spell Sir Winston's practice as First Lord of the Admiralty in 1940, while conducting the grave affairs of the Royal Navy during the North Sea battles of the Norwegian campaign, to spend an hour or so in the afternoons or the early morning completing his chapters on the Norman Conquest and medieval England in *A History of the English-Speaking Peoples.*

Naval signals awaited attention, admirals tapped impatiently on the door of the First Lord's room, while on one occasion talk inside ranged round the spreading shadows of the Norman invasion and the figure of Edward the Confessor, who, as Sir Winston wrote, 'comes down to us faint, misty, frail'. I can still see the map on the wall, with the dispositions of the British fleet off Norway, and hear the voice of the First Lord as he grasped with his usual insight the strategic position in 1066.

But this was no lack of attention to current business. It was the measure of the man with the supreme historical eye -- the distant episodes were as close as the mighty events on hand; the present was illumined by the vision of the past. The procession on the road from Hastings to Narvik and Dunkirk had marched in majestic progress along a predestined course, and it was no accident that on that April day of 1940 the leader of the cavalcade, in its long journey through the centuries, riding unflinching at its head, should be none other than Sir Winston Churchill.

General Eisenhower's Memories
of Churchill
A television interview with WALTER CRONKITE

This programme which was first shown on CBS Television on 24 January 1965 was afterwards shown by the BBC

A few hours after Churchill's death General Eisenhower was interviewed by Walter Cronkite for the Columbia Broadcasting Corporation on television.

CRONKITE: When did you first meet Mr Churchill?

EISENHOWER: I saw him first briefly and at a distance in December 1941 when he came over to meet with President Roosevelt; when I met him first was about June 1942. He came over to visit the President and I had just been named to go to England to command in Europe. So I as the prospective commander called on him at the White House. He was ensconced in a great big bed – later we called it the Queen's Chamber, because that's been a traditional name. And there he was working and I went in and took along with me General Clark and we had quite a chat. And it was very interesting – a very interesting thing particularly because the Allied fortunes were at about their lowest ebb, but this man showed no pessimism, he was talking about plans for winning. It was a very remarkable meeting.

CRONKITE: Did it surprise you that the interview was held in his bedchamber while he was in bed?

EISENHOWER: Well, it was the first hint I got of the unusual daily schedule he kept up apparently all his life. And it was quite inconvenient for staffs that have regular working hours like most of us, because he divided his day into two parts, and I learned to meet with him once in a while – he'd be in bed and I would come in on a busy ten minutes to interview with him – to talk to him for a few minutes.

CRONKITE: What was this schedule of his?

EISENHOWER: When he waked up in the morning he would get his secretaries in and begin to dictate and he'd go through all his despatches. This is during war I'm talking about. His despatches over the night would be in a locked box and he himself had the key and he'd unlock it and read the messages that had come in from all fields. And he would stay in bed till along about 10.30 – something of that time – but meantime working. Now he'd be up until about I suppose two o'clock – or a little later, say almost three. Then he'd go to bed again, and he'd go to bed from three and he'd be up toward evening when apparently he always had a short game of cards with Lady Churchill. It was a two-handed game – I never could understand it – and then he'd start working again about dinner time, and he had lots of dinners that were for business, and would stay up till about 2.30 and then he'd go to bed. So he said it was only proper to divide the work day in two parts, of which one part was from about 10.30 or 11, to up till 2 or 2.30, and the other part the middle of the daylight hours. And I would tell him, I would say, 'Well now, that's all right for you, but I've got staffs that have to be working all day long and I have to be there'. Well, he never did accept our idea of working. But British staff officers, just to keep them going, would have to sleep much later in the morning than we would because otherwise they'd have been exhausted. And so we never tried to talk to them except in emergency before about 9.30 or 10.

CRONKITE: What time would you start your days?

EISENHOWER: Oh, about 7.30. I've always had this habit. Even in the White

With General Eisenhower in England, 1944 (photograph shows him demonstrating his zip 'siren-suit' to the General)

House days I would go to office by 7.45. But in the war I'd always be in my office at 7.30.

CRONKITE: Sir Winston would summon you to meet him at late hours of the night?

EISENHOWER: Sometimes. When I was in London, before Operation Overlord, he liked to go down to Chequers for the weekend. And then he would ask us down, not always, but frequently, for the weekend. And then for those Friday and Saturday nights he would be up till about 2.30. I finally protested and told him I couldn't take this as long as he could, in the same way he could, and finally he agreed that he'd never ask me down except in emergency, after 9.30.

CRONKITE: Were you talking business all that time or was there a great deal of socializing?

EISENHOWER: Oh, at Chequers, the evening would be this: before dinner we'd take a walk, then you'd come in and have a fairly late dinner, and about ten o'clock there would be a – what he called a cinema – a movie picture. And that was when we'd start to work. Maybe we started the picture about 9.30, it would be close as I recall it about 11 when we would start working. Sometimes he'd summon quite a big staff, he'd have a whole roomful of people. They'd have to drive back to London during the night, but about half a dozen of us would stay there till Sunday evening or Monday morning.

CRONKITE: How did his British staff react to these hours?

EISENHOWER: As I say, they had to accommodate themselves and they just had to sleep early in the morning. But they'd come to me and say, now look, General, we can't cross this man; of course we all admire and respect him highly, and have great affection for him. But they just didn't see why they had to work till 2.30 at night. And so they would ask me to begin to suggest some little different arrangement because they said you being Americans you can't incur his anger, but we can. And so he and I, let's say, conversed about the thing, but I'll say this, I don't think he changed his own habits a bit, but he did finally and gradually stop making such terrific demands upon his staff. But the relief was only, let's say, partial.

CRONKITE: How was he towards his staff – did he become angered easily?

EISENHOWER: No, he could get annoyed: if he'd had an idea, he'd want to push it very hard. And if he'd find his staff almost unanimously against it then he would be very annoyed and this was when he would be his most interesting. Because he could show everything from humour to pathos, he could almost automatically turn on the tears, and just show what things would happen if they'd begin to fall to pieces as he would picture them. And he was very difficult – he'd cite history, and all the rest, and then it was difficult to combat him, when he really went into a tense period of argument and urging, and you had to be on your toes to pick out the faults in his chain of reasoning. But he never once failed in his personal courtesy toward the people around him; he respected them and their views; and it wasn't a matter of being cruel or mean about the thing. He just kind of made them see that they were being foolish in opposing him.

CRONKITE: Did he at any time ever threaten to resign his office if he didn't have his own way?

EISENHOWER: I remember he used an expression once; he was talking about a possible operation and he began to build possibility on possibility, and possibility; and then he said if these possibilities came about that would mean a complete destruction of our hopes and in which case I should have to lay down the mantle of my high office. But this was just a remark as going in argument. He had no more intention of resigning than I ever had – than anyone could have.

CRONKITE: You never took that as a serious possibility?

EISENHOWER: No. As a matter of fact the man was too dedicated to his job; he was really, as I thought, the embodiment of all that was best in the British Empire at war. He was a man with a manner of great courage, indomitable will, and he also had with this a great skill of keeping people together; even when they would get weary and worn out on some of these meetings I tell you about, still they recognized that here they were in the presence of a great man who was doing everything for their country and they supported him very gallantly and thoroughly. So he had not only the determination, as you may say, of a bulldog but he had with it a very great skill in personal leadership.

CRONKITE: You mentioned that he rode a destroyer in Operation Dragoon; I remember that he was thwarted from doing that in the D-Day landings in Europe.

EISENHOWER: He wanted to go along and of course everybody else could understand and sympathize with his desire. But I felt that his value to the Government and to the whole Allied cause was so great that we shouldn't take any unnecessary chances with him. And while he had a stratagem to overcome my objections, when the King heard about this intention of his, it was easily defeated because the King said, well I ought to go along too, and then of course the Prime Minister didn't want the King endangered, so they didn't go on that first day.

CRONKITE: What was the stratagem?

EISENHOWER: Well. The stratagem was that he said to me: 'General you are in charge of the operation.' 'Yes.' 'In other words you have your orders on directing the tactical part of this whole affair unquestionably.' 'Yes.' 'But you do have nothing to do with the composition of the crews on His Majesty's ships?' 'No, none at all, that's not my business.' 'Well, then I can sign on, as a member of the crew of [whatever the ship was], and,' he said, 'you could have no objection to my going.' And I said, 'Now look, Winston, you know very well that you can do this. And I know it. But you're going to make my burden heavier if you do.' But still I think he would have gone except for this other intervention.

CRONKITE: Was he an amusing dinner companion at these meetings?

EISENHOWER: Yes; before the time came to discuss the business of the evening, he was one of the most charming men to be with I've ever known. He could tell stories, nearly always about himself — when, I mean, he was sort of the butt of his joke. I'll never forget, he told a story once about the time when he had been fond for a while of a drink named Kummel, and apparently this looks exactly like water. And one day he thought the waiter had brought him a drink of Kummel, and he picked it up and drank it, and he said you know, I had it all despatched before I suddenly found out it was nothing but water, and . . . water, he said, you don't notice. I used to go inspecting around England in a special train and occasionally he went along with me. It happened during dinner that someone used the expression we so often used: 'Shoot if you must this old grey head . . .' Without the slightest hesitancy, he leaned back and started reciting the whole epic poem of Barbara Frietchie, and while he once or twice during the long recital hesitated for a word, he went right on and he not only amazed all of us, but I think all of us were a bit chagrined that none of us could have possibly repeated more than five or six lines of the whole poem. He knew every word of it. He was a many-sided person: all I'm trying to prove is his many sides; he would enliven a dinner conversation with incidents of that kind, and he would pause right in the middle of the soup or something else to make a long quote.

CRONKITE: Was he a good listener?

EISENHOWER: Yes. When someone else had an idea to present or a story to tell he was a good listener. The man was a remarkable individual – indeed I'd like to have the words to express really the depth of the loss I feel right now, in having to recognize that no longer will I be able to communicate with him. I have a vast correspondence with him, because we seemed to take to each other, as the expression is, from the beginning. All during the war, all during my political experiences with him, it was just a great privilege to be talking to him, even when you had your differences. And some of them I know were very harsh and some were strong; opinions very strongly held, they were diametrically opposite, but that's to be expected between strong-minded men, that's all there is to it.

CRONKITE: Did your relations change at all with him or his attitude toward you after you became President of the United States?

EISENHOWER: Oh, no. He no longer I think, would call me 'Ike' all the time, he'd now say 'Mr President'. He came back into the premiership in October, I think it was, of '51; then a little over a year later I went into the Presidency, and even before I was inaugurated, but after being elected, he came over to see me, and we had long talks in New York, in his friend's house, that of Bernard Baruch. Bernard Baruch was one of, I think, his oldest American friends and they were very close all during the years. And it was a great treat to have been there at such a conversation.

CRONKITE: Did you seek, or did he offer, any counsel when you were making your great decision to enter politics?

EISENHOWER: After I finally said in an unguarded moment in early 1952, I'm a Republican, then he said to me, he said, well you're almost certainly going to be the nominee. I said, well I don't know, I hope not. But then when I finally went over to England to tell him what had happened he said well, personally I believe you're going to be nominated and elected, and I look forward to our association. He didn't give me any advice about our elections or how we should conduct them. I did hear him speaking to another person, as a matter of fact to Anthony Eden, talking about the techniques of making a public speech, and it was one of the most interesting moments at a dinner conversation. And really it was almost extraordinary. He said you have to wear glasses? He said get the darkest and thickest rims you can find. He said take them off and use them as something to gesture with, to point with, put 'em back on. You use notes? Tell 'em, put them in your fist, shake them in their faces, don't try to sneak these things off one page with another like there's no notes there. He said, they know you're using them, so show them. He talked for I think twenty minutes or so on the technique of making a public speech. Eden was sitting on my right and the Prime Minister right across the table, and, you know, he was making all these gestures and everything. He was looking at me and at Eden; I had an uneasy feeling maybe he was talking for my benefit too. I didn't know. But he was: he did it for some purpose. He never did anything without a purpose and I'm quite sure as long as he'd known Eden, he'd already given him a lecture on public speaking in the past. Sometimes I had a suspicion that it might have been for my benefit.

CRONKITE: Did it stand you in good stead?

EISENHOWER: Well no, I don't think so. I've never been a public speaker, but he was and he studied the technique.

CRONKITE: Churchill had a great facility for attention to detail, we know. Was he a good military man?

EISENHOWER: Well, he read military history all his life and, of course, he had been a junior officer in the British services years back. He always thought about detail. He thought about the men and the people. One evening, at Chequers, we had quite a large meeting and it included the technician responsible for transporting the military personnel and supplies. Now, the British Staff custom is to refer to all the people they have to carry just as bodies because they don't care whether you're a general or you're a private – they have to carry you and that's that. So, in this exposition that this technician was giving – and the Prime Minister I must point out was not in a very pleasant mood because the statistics given were showing that one of his ideas was impracticable – it happened that this man used this word 'bodies'. He said: 'We have room for so many thousand bodies'. The Prime Minister: 'Wait a minute, young sir, you said "bodies". What way is that to talk about British soldiers?' He said, 'You were talking like they were dead and ready for their coffins'. He said, 'It's inhuman, I won't have it'. He went along this way for about five minutes and the technicians just avoided the word 'bodies'. They had to, but I must say I felt exactly like the Prime Minister about the thing. Whenever they talked and said 'bodies' I sort of jumped. I didn't think it was the way to talk about soldiers and men that were fighting your wars for you.

CRONKITE: He expressed to you, during the war, a concern about Soviet domination of Eastern Europe?

EISENHOWER: Not so much in the early days, but by '44 he was talking that way. And another man who'd got word to me all the time to watch it was a Mr Forrestal. I think Mr Forrestal in our country was always alarmed about that and I would get messages and words even before I'd met Mr Forrestal, at least until I knew him well. Churchill was quite concerned and I think he believed that our government was too ready to take Russian promises at their face value. However, the suggestion was never put in official records. This was the kind of thing he would talk to us about sometimes during these meetings.

CRONKITE: At Yalta did he and President Roosevelt have any really bitter discussions about this?

EISENHOWER: Both those old men recorded one instance. Stalin said that they would probably have to execute at least fifty thousand war criminals. This horrified the Prime Minister and he just said the British people could not be a party to any such blood-letting and that kind of unjust procedure. And he never would agree to it. Mr Roosevelt, reporting the same instance, in exactly the same terms, said, 'Well, I felt this was getting a little embarrassing so I proposed a compromise. We wouldn't shoot more than forty-nine thousand rather than fifty thousand'. The President made a great big joke of it: he had no idea of agreeing to this at all, but he didn't want any difficulties right there between them on this point because, after all, it was just rather a pointless and casual remark. But the Prime Minister took it very seriously. He said he was going to be no party to such a thing. He said let the people, who were judged by their peers to be guilty, be punished but let's go no further than that. So that's the only incident that both of them reported to me about that particular thing. The President, as he came back from Europe, visited my headquarters for two or three days and he told me about it, and then, some time later, it was reported to me by the Prime Minister.

CRONKITE: At Chequers there was a certain formality in these meetings. I seem to remember something about having to sign the 'guest book'.

EISENHOWER: Walter, I think every time I visited any large British headquarters or any home, for any reason, there was always a custom, a British custom, of signing the 'guest book'. At Chequers you signed every time you went in or came out. One day I was rushing from London down to Portsmouth and Chequers was on the way, so I stopped for about ten minutes, it was about nine or ten in the morning and the Prime Minister was still in bed and I ran up to his bedroom and we got our business done and I didn't even sit down. I rushed back and was just getting in my car when I felt a presence round me. And here was a very dignified British butler and he said: 'Sir, the book'. I shot back; the book was fortunately just inside the door; and I signed it and it turned out that the butler was all smiles. I was in the car – gone.

CRONKITE: Was Churchill a great user of the telephone or did he prefer to write?

EISENHOWER: He would use the telephone once in a while. He had a good deal of faith in what we used to call the 'scrambler' during the war. It's a telephone that gets everything all messed up during transmission but it comes back into your ear perfectly good. And he would call me up all right, but never on anything that was truly secret. With truly secret things he would send special messengers or ask me to come and see him or, on occasions, he would come to my headquarters.

CRONKITE: How did he react when he was defeated in the election of '45?

EISENHOWER: I know that he was bitterly disappointed. But out of that came one little incident that I'll always prize very highly. About this time we had no longer an Allied Force. I was Commander of the American Zone and Montgomery of the British Zone, and so on. Suddenly I got a message from him. I think if I remember, it was by telephone. He said could I put him some place down on the Mediterranean where he could work and rest? He said: 'I'm very tired and I'd like to go down and paint and just amuse myself and rest awhile.' I said: 'Of course I will.' Strangely enough, there had been some houses that had been commandeered; they were for rest areas for men and officers and so on. That day we were turning one back and I just got this message. I said: 'Hold that.' I put some things in the house I knew he'd like and so on and sent him down there and he stayed for two or three weeks and was very grateful. The point of it is, he turned to his old American friends who had the power in fact to do this, and I always felt that that was one of the proofs that he really considered me one of his good friends.

CRONKITE: Was he the one who inspired you to take up painting?

EISENHOWER: He used to talk to me about it and I suppose at least subconsciously he did. Because he told me about the great pleasure he got out of it. So in about 1948 as I was getting out of the Chief-of-Staff's office in Washington . . . I began one day, as I was watching a man paint a portrait of my wife. I got myself some paints and began to fool around, and even to this day, I do a little bit of it presuming I have the daylight hours to do it. But anyway the great satisfaction he got out of it did come to my aid when I got a little discouraged; because I never had a lesson in art or painting, and almost all I know about is linear perspective which comes from an old education in a technical school. But it has been a great pleasure for me and it was for him. About four or five years ago he sent over to this country thirty paintings that were exhibited in a number of spots here. They went on to Australia and so on and when they came back to the United States he sent me a message for me to take my choice as a gift from him. I have it and it's in my office now in Gettysburg and it hangs there where everybody can see it that comes up to my office.

CRONKITE: Did he ever do a critique on any of your paintings?

EISENHOWER: He did a funny thing. I suppose, if you can call any of mine a fair thing – as good a thing as I ever did, was a portrait of Winston. I'd found a

photograph that had intrigued me and I painted it. At that time, I was a patient
– I think it was the operation at Walter Reed – and they all sent asking me whether
they could have one of my paintings so I gave this one. When Churchill came
with me, some years later, to visit Dulles, Senator Dulles, who was then in the
hospital, he saw this, and I said: 'Good picture, Winston.' 'Yes, not bad.' And I
said: 'Well that's one of *my* efforts at painting': I was a little cautious. He said:
'Not bad, not bad.' That's the nearest he came ever to giving me a compliment on
my work.

Sir Winston Churchill in old age: study by Karsh of Ottawa

'Le John Bull jovial'

by RENÉ MASSIGLI, G.C.V.O., (HON.) C.H., Commissioner for
Foreign Affairs, French Committee of National Liberation, 1943–44;
French Ambassador to Great Britain, 1944–1955

ENTRE tant de souvenirs comment choisir?

*Broadcast in the
BBC French Service*

Evoquerai-je la première visite que je fis à Downing Street le 9 février 1943?
L'entrevue dura près de deux heures et elle fut mouvementée. Winston Churchill
ne voulait pas seulement ce jour-là être renseigné de première main, par quelqu'un
qui en arrivait, sur ce qui se passait en France; il désirait surtout entretenir le
nouveau Commissaire aux Affaires Etrangères du Comité de la France Libre, des
difficultés qui retardaient la 'réconciliation' du Général de Gaulle et du Général
Giraud, et, à la suite de Franklin Roosevelt, il s'impatientait parce qu'il n'en
comprenait pas les raisons profondes . . . La conversation fut orageuse et je me
souviens qu'à un moment, pour n'être pas obligé d'y mettre fin brusquement, je
fus amené à dire au Premier Ministre: 'Pour moi, qui arrive de France, vous
êtes un second Clémenceau. Si Clémenceau m'avait fait une de ces scènes dont il
avait le secret, je ne m'en serais pas fâché. Faites-moi donc, et aux Français
Libres, tous les reproches que vous voudrez, si injustes qu'ils soient, si cela vous
soulage; je ne m'en fâcherai pas . . .'

Dès ce moment, nous fûmes amis et, dans nos rapports réciproques, ses colères
ne l'entraînèrent plus jamais trop loin . . . Mais je l'avais vu ce jour-là le visage
fermé, les traits durcis, l'image vraie du bull-dog prêt à mordre . . .

L'évoquerai-je quatre mois plus tard, le 4 Juin 1943? Le Comité Français
de Libération Nationale venait d'être constitué à Alger, après trois jours de discussions. Un déjeuner réunissait chez l'Amiral Cunningham, de Gaulle, Giraud,
leurs cinq associés dans le Comité, Churchill, Eden, Macmillan et quelques
autres . . . Dans l'uniforme un peu fantaisiste qu'il s'était attribué et qui le faisait
ressembler à un officier supérieur de la Royal Air Force, il était là, heureux,
épanoui, détendu, débordant d'optimisme, contemplant ces Français, ces amis
incommodes qui lui avaient donné tant de tracas, à qui il avait tout de même fait
confiance au risque de s'attirer bien des désagréments du côté de Washington, et
ce jour-là il était le John Bull jovial, bon vivant, bien vivant . . .

Je le revois deux ans plus tard, le jour de la capitulation allemande. Dans une
ville en liesse, il décida, au cours de l'après-midi, de faire le tour des ambassades

Churchill and his daughter Mary photographed with M. René Massigli, the French Ambassador, when they visited the French Embassy in London in May 1945

alliées, accompagné de sa plus jeune fille, celle qui est aujourd'hui Mrs Christopher Soames, en son uniforme de lieutenant des services auxiliaires féminins de l'Armée. Lui-même arborait ce chapeau de forme étrange, intermédiaire entre le haut-de-forme et le melon que, vers la fin du 19ième siècle, on appelait en France un 'cronstadt' et que l'Angleterre edouardienne avait conservé. Il alla à l'ambassade des Etats-Unis, à celle de l'U.R.S.S.; il vint nous rendre visite dans la charmante maison de Lowndes Place, qui était la résidence provisoire de l'Ambassadeur de France. L'homme, qui avait, dans la victoire finale du monde libre, une part personnelle plus grande que nul autre, venait remercier les représentants des gouvernements alliés du rôle que leurs pays avaient joué dans la guerre et des sacrifices par lesquels ils avaient contribué à la victoire. Et c'était, ce jour-là, le Churchill chevaleresque, à l'âme généreuse, convaincu que la paix était désormais assurée. Au moment de partir – il était déjà dans l'antichambre – on l'avertit que la foule s'était amassée devant la porte pour l'acclamer; je le vis alors tirer en hâte de sa poche un grand cigare, intact bien entendu (je ne connais pas de photographie où il figure avec un cigare entamé). A cet instant, c'était le Churchill que flattait l'encens des acclamations populaires, le Churchill qui aimait soigner son personnage . . .

C'est peut-être à la Chambre des Communes que ce grand parlementaire fidèle à une grande tradition se sentait le mieux dans son élément. Impeccablement vêtu d'un veston noir et d'un pantalon rayé, quand il se levait de son banc et s'approchait de la 'dispatch box' (qu'il fut Premier Ministre ou chef de l'opposition, il n'avait que quelques pas à faire), on le sentait, certes, heureux d'aller à la bataille, mais on devinait aussi en lui l'émotion toujours renouvelée d'être à la place où l'avaient précédé tant de grands ministres de la grande Angleterre. Merveilleux orateur et aussi incomparable artiste, un sens peu commun de la phrase, le souci du mot rare, mais le ton de la conversation, des hésitations, des répétitions, des repentirs, des effets très soigneusement étudiés (de mauvaises langues assuraient qu'il lui arrivait de répéter ses grands discours devant son armoire à glace), l'habileté, pour se tirer d'un pas difficile, à provoquer au moment qu'il fallait, l'interruption qui amènerait de sa part la riposte foudroyante – souvent improvisée à loisir – qui lui rallierait les rieurs des deux côtés de la Chambre. Il possédait au suprême degré l'art du raccourci et des formules bien frappées que l'histoire retiendra – qu'elle a déjà retenues – dur pour ses adversaires, souvent très dur dans son langage, mais sans méchanceté, et les opposants aimaient cet ennemi généreux.

Parlerai-je de l'homme privé dans sa maison du Kent, interrompant la construction d'un mur dont il posait lui-même les briques, pour recevoir ses visiteurs, vêtu de l'étrange combinaison d'aviateur qu'il affectionnait ? Parlerai-je du peintre du dimanche, qui, devant son chevalet, transporté à travers le monde avec lui, de conférence en conférence, oubliait les soucis de la guerre. Vrai peintre ? non, sans doute; mais un amateur de classe honorable et qui savait juger d'un tableau. Je me rappelle un soir, à la Royal Academy, après le banquet, servi dans les salles d'exposition, qui marque chaque année l'ouverture du Salon londonien. Devant un tableau dont l'auteur se croyait justifié par l'exemple de Picasso à déformer et à enlaidir à plaisir la figure humaine, il se retourna vers moi et eut cette simple phrase: 'Picasso, lui, il peut tout se permettre parce qu'il a prouvé qu'il savait dessiner; mais les autres! . . .'

Non, décidément, entre tant de souvenirs, je ne saurais choisir. On ne choisit pas parmi les trésors qu'offre à l'observateur ami une personnalité de cette vigueur, de cette richesse et de cette envergure . . . Encore, n'ai-je rien dit du causeur merveilleux et plein d'humour qu'il pouvait être après dîner, entre amis; je n'ai pas évoqué son goût pour les pompes cérémonielles et la joie enfantine que provoquaient en lui uniformes et dorures, ce qui ne l'empêchait pas, à peine s'en était-il libéré, d'être parfaitement simple . . .

En ce moment, je le revois, la dernière fois que nous eûmes, ma femme et moi, l'honneur et la joie de l'accueillir à l'ambassade.

C'était en décembre 1954 – il venait d'avoir 80 ans. Les membres du Corps diplomatique s'étaient réunis pour lui offrir un souvenir et nous avions choisi, pour ce peintre, une délicate sanguine d'Hubert Robert. Doyen de mes collègues, j'avais le privilège de la lui remettre, en présence des donateurs; je saluai en lui, au noms d'hommes venus des quatre coins de la terre, appartenant à des races très diverses, animés de convictions très différentes, un homme de la grande espèce, dans lequel il n'y avait rien de petit, rien de mesquin.

EVALUATIONS

Churchill as Under-Secretary

KEITH KYLE interviewed by CLIFF MICHELMORE

Broadcast in 'Tonight' 28 January 1965

MICHELMORE: In 1905, Churchill was only thirty-one. He had been in the House of Commons barely five years. These would appear to be rather slender qualifications for so important a post as the Colonial Office?

KYLE: But of course he'd fought in some of the Colonies. I've been going through a lot of Colonial Office documents in the Public Records Office for a book I'm writing and when one comes across him in office the political minutes – minutes written on documents in ordinary ink are by officials; those in red ink by Ministers – suddenly the ministerial minutes positively leap out of the page.

MICHELMORE: But his previous colonial experience had been largely military, hadn't it? – fighting the Dervishes in Omdurman and tribesmen in the North-west frontier. Was this the best training for an Under-Secretary of State for the Colonies?

KYLE: Curiously enough it was. He had been on punitive expeditions. He knew what they were like. He'd also, just before becoming Under-Secretary for the Colonies, changed parties and he was keen to show himself a radical Liberal. For example, take this document. This is a punitive expedition, which has been set in Kenya against a tribe called the Kisii. Now the usual report comes in about the number of Africans killed, the great success of the expedition and recommendation for awards, and he immediately notes in his red ink, 'I do not like the tone of these reports. 160 have now been killed without any further casualties on our side. It looks like a butchery, and if the House of Commons gets hold of it all our plans in East Africa will be under a cloud. Surely it cannot be necessary to go on killing these defenceless people on such an enormous scale?'

MICHELMORE: But at the time his experience of administration must have been negligible. When he came up against the rather ponderous machinery of Whitehall who in fact won in those early days?

KYLE: Well, he usually won. There was one thing that happened to be current when he took office – the abolition of the legal status of slavery in the last piece of East Africa where it was still legal, in the coastal strip around Mombasa. And some official said it would take three years to organize the whole thing. Churchill put in an immediate minute: 'This is most disquieting. Such delays as are suggested would never be accepted by Parliament. I cannot impress too strongly the serious character of the attacks which this case would justify being made on us unless we're able to terminate the slavery status at once.' And he got it terminated at once.

MICHELMORE: In 1906 Churchill introduced the Bill for the rather new and enlightened constitutional scheme for South Africa, but thirty years later he was bitterly opposing the schemes for India Home Rule. Now had he in fact forgotten the lessons of his youth or had he relearned lessons, or learned new ones?

KYLE: I think in some ways he had forgotten the lessons of his youth. When he first went to East Africa, for example, when he was Under-Secretary for the Colonies, he was very liberal in his outlook. For example, he wrote: 'It will be an evil day for these native races when their fortunes are removed from the impartial and august administration of the Crown and abandoned to the fierce self-interest of a small white population'. By 1921, when he became Colonial Secretary, he was taking a much more conservative line. On the other hand, there was a certain element of consistency, I suppose, in that he held throughout that the impartiality of the Crown would maintain justice as between the various tribes.

However, I can't help looking back at something that he wrote on South Africa, a minute, at the time when as Under-Secretary for the Colonies he was piloting through the House of Commons, or proposing to, the Bill which gave magnanimous settlement to the Boers. 'Halting at a halfway house midway in the valley is fatal. What we might have given with courage and distinction both at home and in South Africa, upon our own terms, in the hour of our strength, will be jerked and twisted from our hands without grace of any kind, not perhaps without humiliation, at a time when the Government may be greatly weakened.' If at the age of thirty-one, Winston Churchill had become Colonial Secretary, say when Iain Macleod became Colonial Secretary, I have the feeling that this is the same way he would have reacted to our colonial problems today.

MICHELMORE: May I now give you a quote: 'Clarity and cogency can be reconciled with a greater brevity' was one of his famous admonitions in the Second World War. Now in 1905 he'd just produced – what? a three-hundred-thousand word? – biography of his father. Was this liberality with words evident in his Colonial Office days?

KYLE: I would think he made many more minutes than junior Ministers before him had written. Nevertheless they were clear and cogent, and one thing that he is recorded as having said during this period makes one think forward to the period of the Second World War. Gandhi was received by him in 1906. Churchill was Under-Secretary for the Colonies. Gandhi, also at the beginning of his career, was defending the interests of the Indians in South Africa. And Gandhi reports that when he was received by Winston Churchill, Winston Churchill said to him: 'Please put down your views on one sheet of foolscap'.

Historical Parallels

J. H. PLUMB, Vice-Master of Christ's College, Cambridge,
interviewed by MAGNUS MAGNUSSON

*Broadcast in
'Tonight'
28 January 1965*

MAGNUSSON: 'He held the Grand Alliance together no less by his diplomacy than by his victories. His comprehension of the war extended to all theatres and his authority alone secured design and concerted action. He animated the war at sea no less than on land. He was for six years not only the Commander-in-Chief of the Allies but, though a subject, virtually master of England. He was the head of the most glorious administration in her history.' That is a tribute not about Winston Churchill but by him, a tribute written about John Churchill, first Duke of Marlborough, in a preface to Winston Churchill's biography of his ancestor.

This brilliant soldier-statesman of the eighteenth century formed the Grand Alliance to save Europe from the military domination of the France of Louis XIV, and more than two hundred years later his descendant was the mainspring of another Grand Alliance that saved Europe from German domination. How far was Sir Winston Churchill's thinking and military strategy influenced by his sense of history? And in particular by his intensive study of the victorious campaigns of Marlborough? Dr Plumb, to what extent was Churchill consciously aware of the parallel between himself and Marlborough?

PLUMB: Churchill was constantly aware of the parallel between his own age and that of Marlborough. For example, on 13 August 1942, he was in Moscow and the moment he woke up he said, 'This is Blenheim Day' and Blenheim was on his mind for the whole of that day. And then shortly afterwards he went off to North Africa to see Montgomery who had just been given the charge of the African campaign, and Montgomery asked him to write in his book some few words. And Churchill wrote that he hoped that a new Command which had started in Blenheim week would be equally auspicious and victorious, and of course, in a sense, it was.

MAGNUSSON: But how useful to Churchill was this parallel and to what extent did it help or hinder him in his conduct of the war?

PLUMB: The thing I think that was most important for Churchill in his study of his ancestor's campaigns, and also in his study of English history as a whole, was that it gave him an absolute conviction that battles were important, that England had reached a pinnacle of achievement and greatness through victory in war. And of course in 1939 this was rather an uncommon view. Most statesmen, people like Baldwin I suppose, and Chamberlain, were very much more filled with a sense of the frustration and destruction of war. After all, their atittudes had been largely formed through the First World War in which there were no victors, both those who won and those who lost did equally badly and that great holocaust seemed to have settled nothing at all. And I think this had helped to sap the combative spirit and the aggression of the statesmen and politicians of the west. And Churchill was one of the few who still retained this view: that battle could be decisive, that victory could be decisive, and that victory could bring renewed greatness and grandeur to his own nation.

MAGNUSSON: But strategically the structure of Europe had changed enormously in the two hundred years. Was Marlborough's conception of the Grand Alliance still accurate enough to be of any use to Churchill?

PLUMB: Of course it hadn't changed all that much. There's really a remarkable parallel between the war that Marlborough fought and, in a sense, the war that Churchill fought. After all, the confrontation was the same. You had a great powerful aggressive nation in the core of Europe that could only be contained by a Grand Alliance surrounding it. No one nation could contain the France of Louis XIV, no one nation could contain Hitler's Germany. There had to be a circle of Allies in order to make it possible to contain the expansive and explosive force of both. So really the basic strategic situation was similar. This Churchill realized and, indeed, he formulated in many ways his diplomacy and his strategy by those considerations.

MAGNUSSON: But Marlborough's wars were essentially European wars. It was all fought in Europe. To what extent could this help Churchill in the conduct of a world-wide war?

PLUMB: I think there is a big contrast here, you know, between his conduct of the European war and the conduct, say, of the Far Eastern war. In the European war he moves with, I think, great certainty. For instance, the way he grasped the hand of Russia immediately Russia came into the war. He had no doubt at all that there should be an immediate alliance. He said he'd ally with the devil if necessary. This was necessary for him because Russia was a gap at that time in 1941; Germany was not contained in the east. So as soon as Russia came in he immediately knew what to do. Whereas when we look at his strategy in the Far East, he is moving with far less degree of certainty. He has all sorts of imaginative ideas like landing on Sumatra, or landing on Java, but by and large they were logistically impossible. They were not based on that same deep historical knowledge or, indeed, on the same sort of geo-historical knowledge which his strategy in the West was based on.

*Blenheim Palace
from the south-east*

*John Churchill, 1st
Duke of Marlborough
(1650–1722): after
Kneller*

In the House of Commons

by E. R. THOMPSON, formerly BBC parliamentary correspondent

SIR WINSTON CHURCHILL would have been great if he had never been in parliament; great as a man of action, as an orator, as a man of letters, as a man simply clothed in his own genius. He was a figure on such a scale that no one institution could contain him. And he himself had moods of impatience with parliamentary routine and detail which caused him to fall short in one limited sense of the ideal of a House of Commons man. Yet there was something about the place which was particularly fitted to set him off; and those who were privileged to watch him day after day on the front bench or at the despatch box probably gained as full a sense of his true quality as any but the most intimate observers.

Broadcast in 'Radio Newsreel' (Light Programme)

What, then, were the characteristics in him that we sensed from the gallery of the House of Commons? First and foremost, courage. The rectangular house, with its opposing benches squarely facing each other, is a place of combat. Into this he fitted perfectly. When German bombs destroyed it and it had to be rebuilt, he powerfully influenced the decision to preserve its old form, for reasons which he set forth in a classic statement. He loved the small intimate chamber in which the two sides looked each other straight in the eye; and he himself as Prime Minister sitting on the Treasury Bench at Question Time with head cocked, hands pendant between open knees as he listened for the next question, had unmistakably the air of the old champion in his corner of the ring waiting for the bell. And in this spirit he fought every round until the very last.

He was not above the battle. He would exchange the fisticuffs of party politics with all comers, revelling in the cheers and counter-cheers, braving the taunts and jeers, and flinging them back. He could be so reckless of formal dignity, so full of gesture and grimace, that the respectable would sometimes be scandalized. This was a misunderstanding. Here was the whole man, ready instantly to commit himself in small things as well as in great. It was possible often, in the smoke and murk of these skirmishes, to catch the glint of the metal of 1940. He would fight, that was certain, but it would be no ordinary battle. For there was a second great quality allied to the courage, and that was imagination. Nothing was more extraordinary than to witness the ease – the soaring majesty – with which he would rise from the dust of the arena to heights of vision, eloquence, magnanimity. And for this too, the House of Commons was the perfect theatre.

After the General Election of 1945, when he fell from power at the peak of his glory, he suddenly had to appear, after years of being Prime Minister, as leader of a badly beaten Opposition. Here was a moment. He met it calmly, chivalrously, in a speech that remained among his minor masterpieces: 'I have great hopes of this House of Commons', he said, gazing at the huge ranks ranged against him, and he meant the words. Here was the sense of occasion, the instinct of the dramatist.

He owed, of course, much to art. The courage and the imagination were those of the warrior, but a warrior wonderfully gifted and wonderfully cultivated. It is common knowledge, and he made no secret of the fact himself, that his set speeches were heavily prepared. He spoke from elaborate notes, at which in his later years he peered closely from time to time through spectacles. This was not a weakness, it was an expression of his great strength. He knew best how to achieve his own effects and he would go about it in his own way. His prepared speeches did not betoken any lack of spontaneous power, as his interrupters often found. To say that he was the greatest tragic actor of our time, and the greatest comic actor too, is not to impugn his sincerity; it is merely to recall the versatility of genius. He was made for public action, public speech, the life of leadership, but to him this was no masquerade. He lived before the House of Commons and before the world, a whole man.

W. H. Auden once wrote that 'private faces in public places are wiser and nicer than public faces in private places'. Winston Churchill never feared to show his private face in anger, in laughter, and even in tears. It is for the world to shed them now.

The resolution presented to Sir Winston by both Houses on his retirement from Parliament in 1964

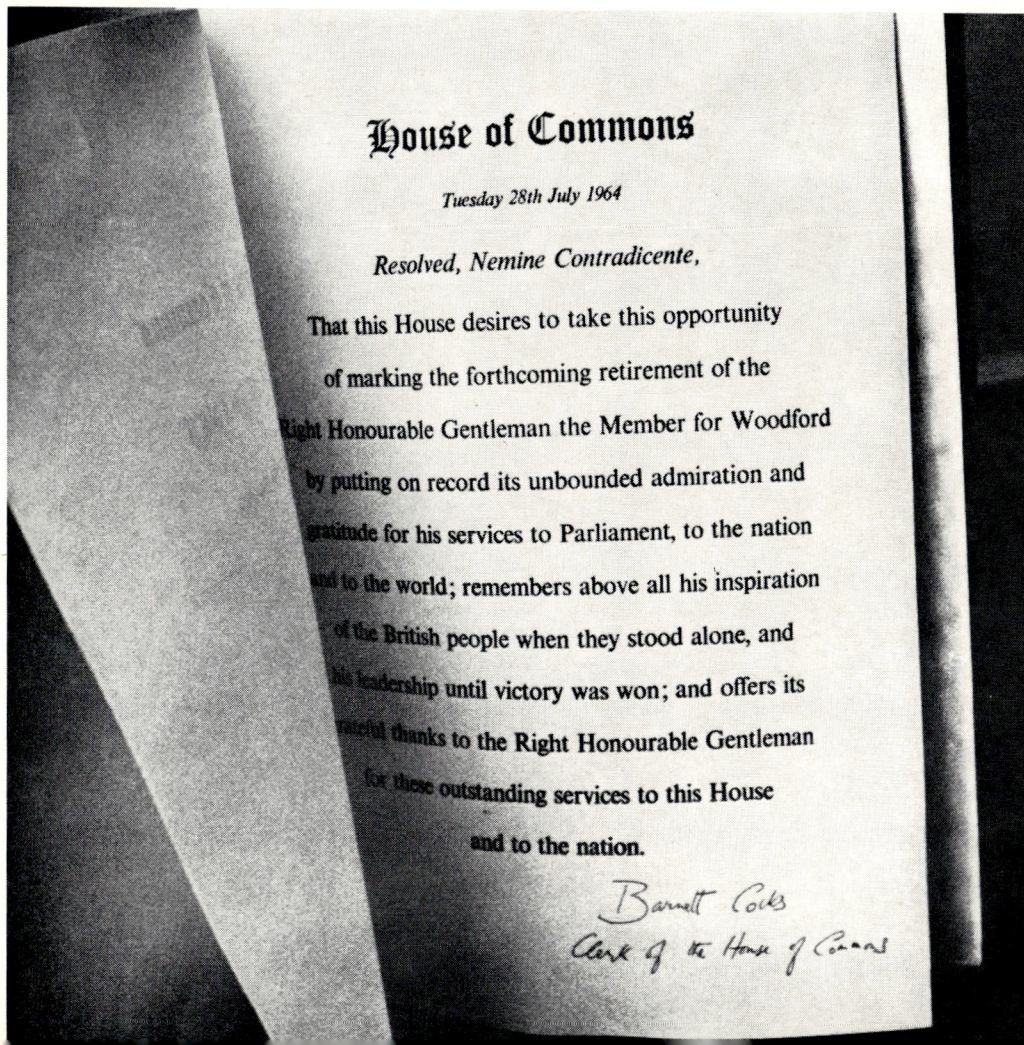

House of Commons

Tuesday 28th July 1964

Resolved, Nemine Contradicente,

That this House desires to take this opportunity of marking the forthcoming retirement of the Right Honourable Gentleman the Member for Woodford by putting on record its unbounded admiration and gratitude for his services to Parliament, to the nation and to the world; remembers above all his inspiration of the British people when they stood alone, and his leadership until victory was won; and offers its grateful thanks to the Right Honourable Gentleman for these outstanding services to this House and to the nation.

Barnett Cocks

Clerk of the House of Commons

Who goes home?

(Winston Spencer Churchill, 1874–1965)

by C. DAY-LEWIS

I

*Broadcast in the
Third Programme*

So the great politician
    Goes home; and we consign
To history his craft of politics
    Ennobled by a vision
    That saw the grand design,
The vaulting arch sprung from the clay-bound bricks.

Soldier, historian,
    Orator, artist – he
Adorned the present and awoke the past:
    Now ended his long span,
    A one-man ministry
Of all the talents has resigned at last.

We knew him in debate
    Provocative or prophetic,
A Puck one day, the next a Prospero.
    We saw him by defeat
    Unsoured – the energetic
Come-back, the magnanimity all through.

Here was a man in whom
    Great issues brought to light
Genius to grapple them. On a poised hour
    Danger drew steel and gloom
    Struck fire from him: the tide
Of battle charged his impetuous mind with power.

So he becomes a myth,
    A dynast of our day
Standing for all time at the storm's rough centre
    Where he, a monolith
    Of purpose grim and gay,
Flung in the waves' teeth the rock's no-surrender.

II

That myth we cherish now the man is dead.
But, living, what was he to most? – a trite
    Cartoon of grit and wit?
A bulldog mouth, a tortoise thrust of the head,
A cigar, a genial snarl? Go deeper. See
    The versatility

Rare in this narrowing age. His soldier's nerve,
Painter's colour-struck eye, orator's flair
    For passion, writer's care
In the menage of thought – all went to serve
His need that life be a momentous tale
    Heroic in scope and scale.

The route was difficult, and the peak remote.
A dunce at school, an uppish subaltern –
    How few could there discern
One who would make the history he wrote?
Or see the young fox-haired firebrand of debate
    Steadying a shaken State?

Aristocratic temper, in an age
Restive against the uncommon, rides for a fall.
    Wilful, mercurial,
Impatient of the reckonings that engage
Small minds, unseated often, still he rose
    Above his falls and foes.

Great Marlborough in his heart, upon his tongue
Gibbon's long thunders, always he foreknew
    High destiny, and grew
Into his legend slowly; then among
Titanic storms claimed an immortal part –
    Gave Britain tongue and heart.

III

    Who goes home? goes home?
    By river, street and dome
The long lamenting call echoes on, travels on
    From London, further, further,
    Across all lands. The Mother
Of Parliaments is grieving for her great, dead son.

A soaring spirit vaults
The failures and the faults
Of the day that it worked in, the will it clarified.
Though a voice is taken hence,
Its reverberant eloquence
Rings on into the ages, rings out on freedom's side.

Remember at his passing
That finest hour – the bracing
Of nerve, the hearts lifting, the challenge to dismay,
When a nation took cheer
From the vision he held dear
Of uplands shining out beyond a sombre day.

But also call to mind
With what grace he resigned
The habit of power, the pulse of action. Character stood
The test of letting go
What had sustained it; so
He and his fame ripened in autumn quietude.

Who goes home? A man
Whose courage and strong span
Of enterprise will stand for ages yet to come.
Storm-riding heart now stilled
And destiny fulfilled,
Our loved, our many-minded Churchill has gone home.

APPENDIX

The world writes of Churchill

by TANGYE LEAN, C.B.E., Director of External Broadcasting, BBC

An article originally published in *The Listener and BBC Television Review*

THERE ARE, of course, two degrees of stature in great political figures: those who transcend their national setting, like Washington and Lenin, and those who keep within it, as Gladstone or Disraeli or Stalin kept within it, in spite of their impact on remote peoples. Moreover, the strength of the national characteristics in a great statesman has the appearance of limiting his claim to world status, so that Churchill's Englishness, his archaisms of manner and vocabulary, seem at first sight to confine him within Anglo-Saxon boundaries.

The letters which reached the BBC from sixty countries about broadcasts on his final illness and death, point at once to characteristics which, on the contrary, made a universal appeal. They came in great numbers from the 'enemy countries', in German, Italian, and Japanese, as well as from all over the Commonwealth. The Indians and Pakistanis, whose independence he resisted, have written as many as the French and the Czechs, for whom he was ready to go through the fire. There have been over a thousand letters in all. The grief in most of them has been personal. It has that characteristic of mourning which shows itself in a deep identification with the dead man. Ghanaians, Nigerians, Indians, and Jews have the feeling that Churchill stood beside them and has now become part of them. They remember key phrases, above all that he would not surrender, and they convert the debt owed by so many to so few to him personally. Letters from a dozen countries do this independently of each other: 'Never in the field of human liberty,' writes a Ghanaian, 'has so much been owed by so many to a single Briton.' The writers are mostly young; they feel Churchill was young, and they have none of the Englishman's sense of inevitability about his death. 'He had kept his inner youth,' writes a Japanese from Tokyo. 'I was surprised to hear he was ninety.' The majority do not understand English. Fifty write in Hausa.

A teacher in southern India, who writes in English, explains how he acquired it:

I heard of Churchill for the first time when I was a boy of twelve, way back in 1930. My country was under the British then, and many Indian nationalists were speaking (and rightly too) of Churchill as a diehard who stood in the way of independence. . . . At school British History was a compulsory subject, but Winston's stock rose high when I was introduced to his illustrious forbear – the hero of Blenheim. From then on I was a Churchill

Broadcasting to the nation from Downing Street

The Churchill Arch, House of Commons (incorporating ruins of the old Chamber)

fan, reading all about him in the few biographical pieces we had in the school library and in magazines. . . . I never saw him, but he made me love the English language. After the war I gave up tea planting and worked for my Master's Degree in English Language and Literature. Today I am a lecturer in English in a college of the Kerala University. I am happy in my job. I owe my happiness to Sir Winston.

The letters started with our first announcement on 15 January: 'Sir Winston Churchill is ill at his London home'. From Pescara in Italy that night, a listener wrote: 'I heard from *London Ultima Ora* of the illness of Sir Winston Churchill. This news has been a great shock to me, as I have heard of his fame since I was a child'. And from La Coruña a Spaniard wrote: 'I should imagine that everybody is very anxious . . . He is the man who protected the freedom of countries'.

As the days dragged on and young listeners had to forgo their pleasure in English pop music, there was nothing but approval for its going. From Czecho-slovakia a dozen teenagers sent letters. 'It was good that you cancelled the programme', wrote one; and another: 'I agree with the great tribute in the *Eroica*.' 'One did not realize that Churchill meant so much to the young generation,' wrote a third. 'Why should it be so?'

Death introduced another phase. 'Though I am in a very remote corner of the world,' wrote a listener in West Bengal, 'a few miles from the Himalayan kingdom of Bhutan, as soon as my wife heard the news of Sir Winston's illness, the whole family's ears were glued every day to the BBC. . . . When the sad news of his death came over the radio, my youngest son cried as if he had lost one of his parents.' Similarly, a listener in Berlin who had been in Palestine in 1940 when he first heard Churchill, declares: 'With so many others I am conscious that I owe him my life'; and an Albanian writes to the Albanian Service of the BBC: 'He liberated the concentration camps, in one of which, Dachau, near Munich, I was. May his name never be forgotten.'

But the sense of gratitude was almost equally intense when it concerns the Churchillian fight for liberty in the broadest sense. More letters came from Spain than from anywhere else. From Madrid a Spaniard writes: '*La memoria de Mr Churchill no se extinguirá nunca en los amantes de la libertad.*' In Catalan another writes from a village near Barcelona: 'We are deeply aware that we owe to him victory over totalitarianism and the wicked men (*els malvats*), although there are still some surviving.' From Barcelona another Spaniard writes: 'His attitude during the world war was the inspiration of humble families and a guarantee of freedom for the Christian men of Spain'; and from Tarragona: 'He was my boyhood hero when the world was in darkness.' A Portuguese, in a small town on the Tagus, simply adds: 'He freed the people and saved the world'.

Germans wrote from Halle, Bayreuth, Greven, Westphalia, Munich, and above all from Berlin. 'We Germans,' says one Berliner, 'should be grateful to Churchill not only for his courage in defeat but rather because he saved us from a shameful Pyrrhic victory, whose consequences would have been more terrible than the quick and catastrophic ending of the German aggressive outburst.' And another: 'It was in the war, when Churchill gave us who were pursued courage, hope, and faith to hold out and not to despair although it often seemed that force and evil must win. It can only be a few who have such a quality of greatness that they can influence a whole world by their example.' A couple from Berlin, Frohnau, write that they will always feel gratitude because 'his brave stand for victory made it possible that life could be lived without tyranny and fear'. 'What impressed us particularly about him,' writes another, 'was his love of truth in speaking to his own people. Where has there been another who could compare with Churchill in this respect?' And from Vienna a Social Democrat writes that Churchill 'will live on in me as a fighter for freedom'.

The letters come from all across Canada, from British Columbia, Alberta, Saskatchewan, Manitoba, Ontario, and Quebec. 'At times,' writes a woman listener in Milestone, Saskatchewan, 'I would get very despondent and then, like a miracle, it seems Churchill would make a speech on the radio and I would feel fine again. To me he was like a massive blood transfusion in a very sick world. In some way his great spirit went out to all of us so that he became part of us and we of him.'

The Australian letters come mainly from the east, from Victoria Point in Queensland to McMahon's Point in New South Wales. From New Zealand, a woman listener writes: 'When his voice came over the radio it seemed so grand and yet so close as though it was meant just for me, here in Christchurch, New Zealand', and another in Auckland: 'He was our rock'.

From Africa, Ghanaians and Nigerians wrote in the language of the Bible. He was Moses. 'I shed my tears as the world mourns the great man, the saviour of mankind'; and a Ghanaian from Accra: 'I think one of the greatest contributions to mankind is for a man not to allow power to make him forget God. At the height of his glory and power, when what he said and what he did brought freedom to all men and women in the world, he never forgot God.'

Letters from the Indian sub-continent are mainly from Ceylon, central India, West Pakistan, and the Punjab. 'From the fifteenth of January,' writes a listener in Dhanbad, Bihar, 'I had been praying and hoping for the recovery of Sir Winston, but God willed it otherwise, and now that all is over and the last great battle lost, something has snapped within me and all seems confusion. . . . Like Job, despite trials and tribulations, Sir Winston's faith in God had never faltered, and God fully rewarded him.'

But as well as these religious feelings, there was the hard issue of race. From Monrovia, in Liberia, an African writes that he is 'sure that if he had not saved the world in the last war, we, who were then children, would have fallen victims to the enemy and not be able to live as free men of colour today. We are the ones that can fully appreciate this wonderful man to our dying day. He was History, and he leaves history for the whole world to read and know who he was, what he did for generations yet unborn'. On the other side of Africa, a Mauritian writing from Vacoas says that 'if a great man of action like Sir Winston had not appeared on the scene of the Second World War, perhaps we would not be living: I say so because Hitler had threatened to get rid of all the coloured people'. And an Egyptian: 'An era of darkness and slavery was about to descend on us at the hands of Hitler and his co-maniacs'.

'Let me tell you,' writes an Israeli from Ramat Gan, 'between our life and death, between inspiring hope and utter despair, there was in those years only one man: Winston Churchill.' Even a Moroccan, in Safi, who 'hates' the English, writes in Arabic to the Arabic Service: 'If fate enables me to be by his grave, I will pray for him and express sorrow at his mistakes'. And another from Casablanca: 'He gave heart and hope to those listeners who, like me and my family, lived under the tyranny of the Vichy régime in Morocco'.

Letters were posted from almost every corner of Malta and from the islanders now dispersed. Mrs Tonna, in Michigan, U.S., remembers 'the times when, half starved, hopelessly surrounded and reduced to nothing, we stood and held and listened to the voice of Winston Churchill in the air from the BBC, giving us courage. . . . That man was a father to us, and his loss meant to me more than the loss of one of my folks, almost. Pray the Lord give him a front row seat in heaven'.

From France, letters came from Amiens, Calais, Cannes, Dieppe, Nanterre, Soissons, Aix les Bains, Chaville, Jambes, Lannion, Bourg, Lyons, and above all from Paris. A Parisian listener was in the Champs Elysées on 11 November 1944, lost in the crowds after the liberation of Paris. She hoped to see de Gaulle by paying twenty-five francs for a place on a ladder. 'A great roar came up from the direction of the Concorde – "de Gaulle is coming", we thought. The roar grew until for a moment I thought the building behind us had been bombed and was coming down – because the war was still on. But no; the building was still there in front of me, and to my amazement I saw that it was – Churchill! Churchill and de Gaulle – Churchill! I didn't know that he was in Paris.' And the writer prays that the Entente Cordiale will come to life again and live for ever. Her wish is reflected in a collection of precious R.A.F. leaflets sent to us by a listener who declined to hand them in to the Kommandatura in Soissons, and by a great number of little mourning cards sent as to a close relative.

On Saturday, 30 January, the day of the funeral, it was still night-time in Canada. 'When the BBC broadcast began,' reports our correspondent, 'it was only half an hour after midnight in the wilderness of the Yukon, half-past one on Saturday morning in Vancouver . . . and half-past five on the Atlantic shore of Newfoundland. But no matter what the time or where, the Canadian Broadcasting Corporation had all its transmitters working, those in the Arctic for the first time at night; they and those of the private stations, well over 300 altogether, French as well as English, were linked to the BBC. . . . I turned the radio on in my home near Ottawa at about twenty-past four, and as I looked out across the dim, snowy landscape, I saw lights coming on in other homes which normally would be dark and sleeping.'

In Australia, meanwhile, it was the evening of a summer day. 'Nearly every national and commercial radio station had arranged to carry the full broadcast from London,' said the BBC correspondent in Sydney. 'Every sound was also travelling still more thousands of miles across this continent, to the lonely home-steads on the cattle stations of the outback, to the sugar plantations of Queensland.'

All over Africa, direct into Europe through the home stations of France, Western Germany, Austria, Italy, Greece, Turkey, and Finland, the funeral broadcasts went on a wider scale in the appropriate languages than any broadcast before. The feelings of the world, as it listened, are now a matter of history. It is the young people who have been moved as much as the middle-aged. It is the people who were themselves threatened by extinction for reasons of race or colour who saw him most sharply as the defender of liberty. If the Commonwealth and the United States saw him close to as their great defender, it was the world which claimed him as its hero.

Churchill's roots were in the past, but he saw the essential thing about it which was contemporary. 'Our ancestors so managed,' he said in the Commons thirty years ago, 'that in the main the special interests of Britain conformed to the general interests of the world.'

Members of the public filing past the catafalque in Westminster Hall as the body of Sir Winston Churchill lay in state, 27–30 January 1965